Carlos's passion for life comes through in this book, inspiring us to not only live in the moment but create the moments that make life worth living.

Ann Voskamp
New York Times bestselling author
One Thousand Gifts

When we look back on our lives, we won't remember watching television or playing video games. We will remember the moments where some kind of love or acceptance was exchanged. The premise of Carlos's book is those moments don't have to be accidental. We can make them happen. I'm grateful he's showing us how.

Don Miller
New York Times bestselling author
Blue Like Jazz

Over the past several years, I've watched Carlos and his family live out the message of this book and I'm honored to endorse it. They see life through a lens that inspires me to be attentive and willing to create marked moments in my life as well as the lives of those around me. Truly, it isn't just a collection of great stories; it's more than that. *Moment Maker* is a book that will change the way you capture life and share it with others, and it will no doubt inspire you to be constantly searching for opportunities to embrace the greatness that blooms in the ordinary. Grab this book with excitement, knowing that you're about to enter into a place where moments will no longer be seen as fleeting, uncontrollable, and short-lived. Instead, they're yours for the taking; better yet—they're yours for the making. Isn't it time you started?

Angie Smith
Women of Faith speaker and bestselling author
I Will Carry You, What Women Fear, Mended,
Audrey Bunny, and *Chasing God*

D0972975

Leaders are moment makers. And memory creators. My friend Carlos Whittaker is a leader who lives out what he believes, puts into practice the idea of cherishing each day, and has assembled a book that is a game changer. What are you waiting on? Seriously. Buy this book. Change your perspective on what it looks like to squeeze the life out of each day!

I've worked together with Carlos the last six years on creating moments at Catalyst, and I'm incredibly pumped that finally "Los" has captured some of his own moments, memories, life stories, inspiration, and wisdom into a kick-butt and take-names, game-changing book that will give you fresh perspective on making the most of your own moments, and creating memories in your own life. Buy this book!

Brad Lomenick
author, *The Catalyst Leader*
advisor and brand ambassador, Catalyst

If you're tired of slugging through the monotony of life and feeling like a spectator in your own story, then *Moment Maker* is determined to fix that. This book is a life-altering, direction changing, apathy-busting invitation to live our lives to the fullest. You can't read it and not be changed. I loved it!

Mike Foster
People of the Second Chance

Carlos Whittaker is a gifted musician and communicator, and I love how his personality is translated in his writing. *Moment Maker* points out the importance of paying attention and seizing the opportunities God has placed in front of us to create memorable moments in our own lives and the lives of others.

Perry Noble
senior pastor, NewSpring Church

MOMENT MAKER

YOU CAN LIVE YOUR LIFE OR IT WILL LIVE YOU

CARLOS WHITTAKER

ZONDERVAN®

ZONDERVAN

Moment Maker
Copyright © 2013 by Carlos Whittaker

This title is also available as a Zondervan ebook.
Visit www.zondervan.com/ebooks.

Requests for information should be addressed to:

Zondervan, 3900 *Sparks Drive SE, Grand Rapids, Michigan* 49546

Library of Congress Cataloging-in-Publication Data

Whittaker, Carlos, 1973–
    Moment maker : you can live your life or it will live you / Carlos Whittaker.
      pages   cm
    ISBN 978-0-310-33797-3 (softcover)
    1. Christian life. I. Title.
BV4501.3.W48 2013
248.4—dc23   2013039708

All Scripture quotations, unless otherwise indicated, are taken from The Holy Bible, *New International Version®, NIV®.* Copyright © 1973, 1978, 1984, 2011 by Biblica, Inc.® Used by permission. All rights reserved worldwide.

Any Internet addresses (websites, blogs, etc.) and telephone numbers in this book are offered as a resource. They are not intended in any way to be or imply an endorsement by Zondervan, nor does Zondervan vouch for the content of these sites and numbers for the life of this book.

All rights reserved. No part of this publication may be reproduced, stored in a retrieval system, or transmitted in any form or by any means — electronic, mechanical, photocopy, recording, or any other — except for brief quotations in printed reviews, without the prior permission of the publisher.

Published in association with the literary agency of The Fedd Agency, Inc., Post Office Box 341973, Austin, Texas 78734.

Cover design: Curt Diepenhorst
Cover photography: Tomas Rodriguez/Corbis
Interior design and composition: Greg Johnson/Textbook Perfect

Printed in the United States of America

---

14 15 16 17 18 19 20 21 /DCI/ 22 21 20 19 18 17 16 15 14 13 12 11 10 9 8 7 6 5 4 3 2 1

To my wife, Heather—
For the moments you could have left, and you stayed
For the moments you could have hated, and you loved.
For the moments you could have despaired, and you hoped.
For the moments you could have destroyed, and you healed.
The face of Jesus never looked better.

CONTENTS

THE MOMENT THAT MADE ME

I remember the moment.

It was wrapped in the scent of Play-Doh and the sounds of Karen Carpenter crackling softly on the record player in the corner of Mrs. Stephens's preschool room in Decatur, Georgia. The air was thick and damp. In that basement of a 1970-something Presbyterian church building, there was no telling what was growing in the corners.

I was a shy kid, a Panamanian/Mexican with an Afro parted down the side like Gary Coleman on his best day in a land of bright blond hair, deep blue eyes, and thick Southern accents.

And it was the day this shy kid dreaded—the day we found out what part we would play in the Thirteenth Annual Rehoboth Presbyterian Church Preschool Circus. The year before I'd been a lion.

I remember being mortified as my scene had come up. *Roar, Carlos. Roar loud. Roar like you mean it. Roar like Adam Shaver roars. No. Roar louder than him. Roar like Adam Shaver wishes he could roar,* I thought, trying to psych myself up.

My classmate Adam was about three times my size and, I swear, at four years old already sounded like his dad.

When the time came for me to roar, I can only describe what came out of me as the sound a kitten makes when you step on its tail. I remember the crowd erupting in laughter and my four-year-old world imploding as I hung my mane in shame.

And I have to do this *again*? Please no.

Mrs. Stephens's eyes were staring down through her brown-rimmed glasses at a forty-five-degree angle, studying the clipboard in her hands. Every so often, she would lift just her eyes and scan the room. My heart pounded.

"Mary Helen Addison ... a dancing bear."

"Brandon Bugg ... a clown."

"Jay Clements ... a muscle man."

She went slowly and meticulously through the alphabet. At this point I was furious that my dad was birthed into the Whittaker family. Couldn't we have been the Andersons or something?

As she worked her way down I noticed all the outgoing kids were getting picked as acrobats and clowns. Then I realized that all the animal parts were taken. Sweet. Maybe this meant I was going to be one of the twelve or so balloons and only had to stand on the stage floating from side to side with no chance of verbally failing.

"Carlos ...," she said. For the first time, she raised her head completely. She took off her glasses ... She smiled a smile that I remember to this day. It was filled with hope, compassion, and security.

"Carlos ... you are going to be this year's Ring Master."

That moment, wrapped up in that one sentence, actually changed everything for me. It changed the trajectory of my very future. It affected where I am even today. As mortified as I was, I was actually empowered. She thought *I* could be the Ring Master. She thought *I* could be the star. She guided me to a moment that defined so much of my future.

And by "so much of my future" I mean third grade. I'm thinking of Matt Breedlove telling me I always get picked last in tag because I'm slow, and I'm thinking of being able to respond to him with a simple smile ... and making him my first victim in that small game of tag.

I'm also talking about eighth grade when I knew in my heart that I would be happy just running for treasurer, but instead checking the box on the application that said "President"—and winning.

It also manifested when I walked in front of forty thousand people to lead them in worship. I was thinking on the way to the platform how I had managed to con my way into this situation only to go into a five-song worship set moments later that was life giving and full of confidence.

Throughout my life, I've defaulted to the assumption that I will play a supporting role; but then that fateful day in kindergarten, when Mrs. Stephens allowed me to believe in something greater than second place, finds its way into my awareness.

My entire existence since then has been an exercise in approaching every moment as an opportunity to make the most of life. It's that simple. And because I've done that, I have spent the last forty years in a life full of adventure.

And the greatest adventure? Getting to take this journey with one beautiful woman and three scraggly ragamuffins. Allow me to introduce you to the Whitts. I guess I am what you would call the idea guy. I come up with harebrained schemes and then make the pitch to Heather.

Heather is my wife and our family's Moment-Making Producer/Director. She is the map that guides our Moment-Making journey. Homeschooling the kids and consistently schooling me, she is the one with the ideas and the vision to make the adventure ... well ... an adventure.

Sohaila is our oldest and the part of my Moment-Making lifestyle that brings the drama—and, I mean $D-R-A-M-A$. Every good story has some. The action flicks. The love stories. Even a romantic comedy wouldn't be complete without some drama. That's Sohaila's job: to bring the drama.

The middle child is Seanna (pronounced *say-AH-nuh*). She's our diva. Every good plot needs this character. Especially when making moments, you have to have that element that makes you believe you are "all that" and then some in order to have the confidence to jump into moments! Seanna brings the spunk, the wit, and the neck roll. You know the roll—the one that Beyoncé does in every single one of her videos. She gives us just enough attitude to pull a moment off.

And last but definitely not least, we have Losiah. Seven million people know Losiah from the "Single Ladies Devastation" YouTube video that went viral, in which I told him he couldn't sing Beyoncé's song because he's not a single lady. He is the swag of the family—the headlining talent. He gets us into exclusive events we could never access without him. Losiah was also the first step we took as a family toward fully living a lifestyle of Moment Making. The moment we stepped off the plane in Korea to pick up this seven-month-old boy, Heather and I looked at each other with the same thought as the kid on the cover of this book:

"Well, either we jump or we turn around ... let's jump!"

All of these characters have made me and helped me make this life. And they pave the way for me to have a job that fits my Moment-Making life as well. I participate in the creative process for experiences that reach thousands. I get to produce moments that will hopefully change people into risk-taking Moment Makers. I also lead worship across the world and help people encounter Christ through a moment in a song. It's a good gig and one that begs me to risk comfort on a daily basis in order to see the face of Christ clearly.

I make moments on a daily basis because I want to know that when life has decided it has had enough of me, it's gonna be because it is exhausted from trying to keep up.

Moments are fleeting, but they can have a huge impact. The experiences we have in those moments, good and bad, are what shape who we are and who we become.

Created, Received, and Rescued

A Moment-Making lifestyle boils down to three basic approaches—Created, Received, and Rescued—and I want to share how they have changed everything about how I live and the choices I make.

Some moments are created by us. In Created Moments we are in charge. We create them so the world around us does not simply exist, but thrives—birthday surprises, engagements, sending an In-N-Out Burger overnight to a friend stuck in Madison, Wisconsin. We get to choose!

Others are received to us. At this point in Moment Making we are not initially in charge. We receive a gift that changes everything—a chance encounter, an unexpected payoff, or a happy accident . . . Received Moments. These provide a shift in our ethos that, whether large or small, affects the trajectory of where we are going.

And then there are moments that must be rescued. Rescued Moments unfold in a way we did not intend yet allow us an opening for growth and change. These are the moments when a failure, whether our fault or not, is in need of revival—sickness in the family, a marriage falling apart, or simply missing the mark. When we can see beyond the moment to the potential, we can turn a disappointment into our destiny.

In each of those moments, we have an opportunity to let them happen to us . . . or let *us* happen to *them*.

Through this book I will share with you some amazing, simple, and unexpected moments. I will open up my life and lay it on the table. You will see some of my biggest successes and some of my most epic failures. And hopefully I can help you take control of this gift of life that we've been given and discover how not to let it pass us by.

At the end of the book I will give you four principles for Moment Making that I believe are essential for getting the most out of this life—*Understanding*, *Exploring*, *Pausing*, and *Living*. The afterword will explain more fully what they mean and how you can apply them to your Moment Making, though you will see examples of them in each of the stories I share as well.

Big moments. Small moments. Amazing moments. Devastating moments.

In all of them, I will direct you to the greatest Moment Maker of all time—Jesus—and use illustrations from his life, his ministry, his messages, and his interactions with everyone he encountered to show you what a life of Moment Making is really all about.

We were created by a God who wants us to live fully alive and on purpose. He gave us a model of how to live this way in Jesus. We are to be engaged and pay attention—just as Jesus was. Always on the lookout for what can be created, received, or rescued. He shows us how—how not to be a Moment Taker, but to be a Moment Maker.

We are put here with a purpose, and that plays out in what we do with each and every moment we draw breath. Maybe you will get some ideas from my experiences; maybe you will learn what *not* to do. But more than anything, I pray you will be inspired to seek opportunities to make moments for yourselves and others every day.

PART ONE

CREATED MOMENTS

Her name was Kate. She didn't have feelings. She didn't care about my family or me. All she wanted were two things: food and water. Kate was our goldfish.

God placed Kate in this world so she could feed bigger fish … with herself.

Yet my family had taken this forty-nine-cent fish and given it a name, a home, and had somehow managed to convince me that taking Kate on our cross-country road trip on the floorboard of our Hyundai Santa Fe was not only a feasible idea, but a good one.

We were on the home stretch. We had kept that fish alive for three weeks as we drove all over this land of our forefathers. We had driven from Atlanta to Los Angeles and everywhere in between, and Kate had survived. I, on the other hand, was not doing so well.

If any of you have ever been on one of those great American tours with your family, you know where I'm going. Somehow this road trip idea has made its way to the top of the list for Moment-Making families everywhere. I'm not sure whose idea it was, but I think it was out of necessity and not out of a love for travel. At some point we began to realize that things and people outside our neighborhoods were worth seeing, and making those journeys with kids and pets in tow was the way it happened. Thus was born the family road trip. Alas, our culture has embraced this form of Moment Making, and, well, seeing that I live to make moments, I get in the car when my wife says, "Get in." I drive ... and a long way.

Growing up in Pico Rivera, California, we had a 1978 Buick Regal, all red, inside and out. All-leather seats and a CB radio mounted to the front dashboard that was my portal to the outside world (which led mostly to truck drivers cursing and telling us jokes that no fifth grader should hear).

"Dad? Are we there yet?"

I slaughtered my dad with this question. Absolutely annihilated him. And he took it like a champ. Now, as an adult, I should be in better control of my responses, but I'm not. On this trip, my kids slaughtered me with that question. Absolutely annihilated me. I took it like a third-grade schoolgirl.

"*No*. We are *not* there yet. We are *nowhere* close. We are so far away that I think we won't make it home until you are at least *fifteen*. You're eight now. Do the math. That's seven more years. So sit back, relax, and enjoy seven more years of *misery* before we get home."

That didn't work. Tears from the kids and a scolding death stare from the wife made that clear. But we were on the home stretch. The last three weeks, no matter how miserable the driving, had actually been peppered with amazing moments. Moments that, had we not piled into that Hyundai Santa Fe, we would never have experienced.

One of the family moments we make sure not to miss is what we like to call the Birthday String. It is a bit of crazy, filled with a lot of fun. The Birthday String consists of this: a string. Epic, I know. But it is a moment we look forward to every birthday.

What happens is that on the eve of the birthday, the family member whose birthday it is hits the hay ... and then we begin laying the labyrinth. We start at the bed of the supposedly sleeping birthday human. (I say human because this isn't just a kid thing. And "supposedly" because they are usually too excited to sleep but play along anyway.)

We attach the string to the bedpost of the sleeping human's bed and start unrolling the spool—across the room, through the ceiling fan, down the hall, into the closet, out the front door, around the backyard, into the kitchen, into the freezer, past the oven, and end somewhere *epic* ... typically the toilet or another place equally odd.

Along this maze we tie surprises to the yarn. Upon waking, the birthday boy or girl will discover, as they follow the string, small presents they get to open along the way. The presents on the string are kinda like stocking stuffers—small, inexpensive, but with lots of thought behind them. We love it. Not only because it's fun to do but because we can take this moment with us anywhere.

On this three-week road trip, we had to celebrate Sohaila's birthday in a hotel room. When she woke up in the morning it looked like a scene out of the horror version of *Charlotte's Web*. The place was completely covered with string. And even though she could see absolutely every present from her bed, we made her follow every inch of that string.

These kinds of moments aren't the monumental, life-changing kind, but the kids look forward to them. What's great is that they look forward to the moment of the Birthday String more than they look forward to the actual presents attached to the string.

And that takes me back to the moment on Interstate 40 East. It had been a great day. We'd been driving for seven hours. We had seen the Grand Canyon, had sung for hours in the car, and had knocked at least a year off of our lives by eating seven pounds of truck-stop snacks. Then I felt the car do something funny. Kinda like if I quickly took my foot off the gas pedal. Except I did not take my foot off the gas pedal.

"Did you feel that?" I asked Heather.

"Yeah. Did you do that?" she replied. I assured her I did not.

We were ninety minutes from the hotel. Ninety minutes from Albuquerque. It did it again . . . this time for about five seconds. *No. Please, God. No. Can I remind you that ninety miles from Albuquerque is not the same as ninety miles from Los Angeles?*

At this point the kids could feel the car tripping out.

"Um, Dad? What's wrong with the Santa Fe?" the seven-year-old asked.

The *Santa Fe!* This old girl was breaking down in her home-land. This was only getting better. Pray. Pray. Pray. Pray. *Please, Lord, get us to our hotel in the big city so we can see what's up with our car. Please!*

As soon as I said amen it was over. We cruised to a complete stop on the shoulder of Interstate 40. Cars flew by us at 90 mph, and I was cursing them for putting my family in jeopardy, only to be reminded that I had been going 93 mph only moments earlier. That was my conscience . . . I mean, wife.

I corralled the family over an embankment and under some barbed wire that led to an access road. And there we sat. Heather and I were meticulously planning our escape when the youngest yelled, *"Kate! Kate is still in the car!"*

In the frenzy of trying to get my family to safety, I had made sure to tell them that if we stayed in the car we could get smashed and killed by a semi that was motoring down the interstate. (Another parenting win by yours truly.) So, in our haste to escape the danger on the shoulder of the freeway, we had for-gotten the forty-nine-cent aquatic creature on the floorboard of the Santa Fe, and the realization of this put my kids in an all-out panic. Heather looked at me like, *You made this bed, cowboy, go sleep in it.* So, through the barbed wire and over the grassy knoll I went—all to save Kate.

As I walked back up the embankment, my family was screaming instructions at me: don't drop Kate; hold Kate's tiny tank by the bottom, not the top; don't sway too much because that may hurt Kate. And for a brief second, just a brief one, I had the thought that since we were already in a state of chaos, why not just lose the fish, suffer the consequences, and not have to drive with this fish anymore. It was only a moment. Forgive me.

I made it back to the family with the fish. By this time we started seeing a few people emerging from the land across the street.

"You guys okay?" they asked.

We had broken down in front of a ranch, and I guess they don't get many visitors. We called AAA and then realized that we were going to have to go back thirty miles to get the car to a mechanic who could look at it in the morning. We just decided to make the most of it and started playing Go Fish on the road.

"Go Fish!" the oldest one yelled.

As I was drawing the card, I caught a glimpse of her face. The New Mexico sun was about fifteen minutes from setting and the reflection in her eyes was stunning.

"Get up!" I yelled.

I sprinted back to the car, grabbed my Nikon, and started snapping. I got some of the most beautiful shots of my girls I have ever captured.

The sun was at the perfect level behind me, and it was lighting them up with a heavenly glow. The New Mexico sun was living up to all the license plates.

First up was Sohaila. She was wearing a camo dress and cow-boy boots. She pranced and pivoted, swinging her head back as if she had been coached in runway modeling. It was quite a show.

Seanna, on the other hand, deliberately tries to be as different as possible from her older sister. She won't smile unless you tell her not to smile, and she wouldn't pose if her life depended on it. But she sure does excel in the stare-down. So I rolled with it and got some great shots that really capture her essence.

That twenty-minute photo shoot gave us more than just great pictures; it gave us a collection of images to build memories on and a way to preserve some of their childhood. It turned into one of the best moments of the year.

The tow truck finally arrived, and we spent the next two days stranded in Gallup. Yeah, I'll go ahead and skip right past that part of our saga.

But in the fast forward, it is important to take away from the story that had we not broken down there, and had we not decided to stop and enjoy the moment playing Go Fish on the side of the road, I would never have been able to capture those perfect shots. We could easily have become focused on mechanics and hotels ...

But then we would have missed the opportunity to preserve the memory of our time together. And that, my friends, is what Moment Making is all about—using time to create a story worth reading. Not everyone is going to write a book about their lives and sell it on bookshelves. But we all write a story through our lives that will be read by those around us. And through that, we have an opportunity to have an impact by touching just one other person. And that, by extension, will change the world.

As you begin this epic journey of making moments, keep these three truths close at hand:

1. Creating Moments Has Nothing to Do with Cash Flow

Sure, having a stacked bank account is fun. But that's almost too easy. In fact, the stacked bank account can actually stifle our creativity when becoming Moment Makers. As the old saying goes: Necessity is the mother of invention.

When you have limited funds, you have to rely on ingenuity and being attentive to what is around you. Anyone can *buy* a moment, but not everyone can *create* a moment. We passed hundreds of places we could have dropped a dime and bought a ticket to go into some museum, go-cart track, or movie theater. But not one of those could have bought the moment created on the side of Interstate 40. Broke and broke down—the setting for a perfect moment.

2. Creating Moments Is All about the *Now* before the *How*

The word *how* can kill your moments … the word *now* will breathe life into them. When we start overprocessing the schematics of a moment, we miss out on the beauty of everyday Moment Making. Yes, huge moments are epic and need planning and strategy, and we will talk about those in this book.

But I'll say it till I'm in my hearse: Life is too big to fit in a bucket. Those bucket lists are fun, but quit staring at the bucket list and start finding the everyday moments that you can create *now*. The *how* will fall into place. I promise.

3. Make Your Moments—Don't Make Theirs … or Mine

There is nothing worse than a copy-and-paste moment. We live in a world filled with YouTube marriage proposals and reality show dreams. God has placed a unique design inside of your heart to make moments unlike any other. Don't cheapen what he has created in you by just carbon copying what is inside someone else.

Throughout this book you will uncover ways of accessing that creativity; but for now, let this symphony of stories inspire you to begin to write your own score. You are the composer, and your symphony of moments is waiting to be heard.

* * *

Quite simply, Created Moments must be created. These are the moments where you put your head down and do the work. Birthdays, anniversaries, reunions are all fun to plan and create, but we also need to consider the in-between—the life that is lived around the *big* moments. Along the way you will find you are *living* a life filled with opportunities to create moments by yourself, for others, and with God. Created Moments.

You are going to learn about my crazy life and how I choose to make the most of it. But I also want you to see how Jesus, the consummate Moment Maker, was doing this every moment he drew breath here on earth. He never missed an opportunity to make a moment teachable. He never passed up a chance to make a connection with someone and touch their lives. Even though Jesus had access to unlimited and unfathomable resources, he worked best with a pretty simple set of tools. He had engagement, he had purpose, and he had love. That was pretty much all he needed … and it's really all you need too.

CHAPTER 1

CREATING VALUE

It was my eighth birthday. For my party I wanted a Scooby-Doo theme. I remember the conversation with my mom.

"Carlitos. What kind of birthday party do you want?"

"I want a Scooby-Doo party."

"Okay. What does that mean?"

"I want Scooby-Doo all over my party."

And I got it. In the gymnasium at Briarlake Baptist Church my dreams came true. Now, little did Carmen know that what her son *really* meant was that he wanted Daphne Anne Blake—you know, the redhead in the gang—at his party . . . not Scooby-Doo.

Actually, I'm not sure I really understood that. At least, not until Chandra Bishop came walking up those stairs dressed up as Daphne Anne Blake. Mama mia! The party went from being a Scooby-Doo party with all of my eight-year-old friends to a roller-skating date with me and Daphne Anne Blake . . . I mean, Chandra Bishop.

The day before the party, my mom took me to Kmart, and we hit the birthday aisle. It was filled with paper plates, cups, streamers, tablecloths, knives, forks, hats, and anything else a parent would need to throw their kid the perfect themed party. And right there, between the Captain Caveman plates and the Punky Brewster cups, was about twenty-five dollars worth of Scooby-Doo goodness. She bought it all. Even the candles were somehow Scooby-Doo. And just like that—we were ready for a Scooby-Doo party.

It was great. Exactly what I wanted. Everybody went home with Scooby-Doo goodie bags filled with Scooby-Doo PEZ dispensers and other junk that would probably end up in the trash. I got to skate around the gym of Briarlake Baptist Church with Chandra Bishop. It almost felt like a real date.

The next year we tried Walmart for another set of plates, cups, and napkins, I'm sure. I don't remember what the theme of year nine was though—either because Chandra Bishop wasn't there or because it reminded me a lot of the year before . . . and the year after.

You see, when we get used to things, we begin to get callous toward them. It is especially true in this age of Pinterest and You-Tube. In fact, a new trend is popping up. It's the "I'm gonna outdo your birthday party" movement.

Maybe this existed in the '80s and I was oblivious to it, but I can't remember all the moms trying to outdo each other in the birthday-party category the way you see nowadays. It's nearly impossible to do a simple backyard party with cake and ice cream anymore. I believe the one-upmanship that is taking over party planning is fueled by social media and cable TV. Have you seen *My Super Sweet Sixteen* reality show?

The pressure to put on a big production is huge. And even I have succumbed to it. But that's because sometimes it's more for us than it is for the person we are supposed to be celebrating. And at times it has the potential to completely derail a moment.

There's nothing wrong with enjoying the beauty of the moment you made for them, just be sure that what you are creating is something they really want and not just something you want for them—or want them to want.

It's a hard thing to do. I think that's why the simplicity of what my generation had growing up was much more powerful than the extravagance of today's rat race to get the most "Likes" on a party you threw for your kid. But don't think I am standing on the outside criticizing. I have fallen victim to this same compulsion.

When my seven-year-old told me she wanted a Taylor Swift birthday party, I figured I was heading to a superstore. She wouldn't have minded at all. All she wanted was to have her friends together ... oh, and a little shopping for the latest eight-year-old-girl craze. But that's it. That's what she wanted. All we needed to do was make sure that happened and we were gold.

Well, about a week before the party, Jenny, one of our close friends, had an idea. She said, "What if you did a Taylor Swift video shoot for the kids?" I could literally see the sparkle in my wife's eyes, and I knew then that I would need to brush up on my video-editing skills. *This was it.*

The anthem the kids had been singing for months, nonstop ... months, nonstop ... months, nonstop ... (get my point?) ... was the song "Mean." It's a spunky, feisty song, perfect for my Seanna. This was the song they would perform for the video. Now for the plan.

If this moment was gonna work, I was going to have to leave Dad Zone and go into Spielberg Mode in a hurry. I knew this much had to happen: all the girls would have to learn all the lyrics ... well, all the correct lyrics. They'd been singing every word they understood for weeks on end. I would have to capture them lip-syncing it in order to get it to sync up with the original song. Easy, right?

The day of the shoot came, and we had all the girls bring cowgirl boots and hats. They all showed up and looked amazing. We corralled the girls into their very own dressing room and makeup studio where we started dolling them up. I mean the whole she-bang. We had makeup artists (moms) plastering their faces with war paint. We had hairdressers (moms) teasing and curling, getting the girls' hair ready for the big shoot.

I, on the other hand, was busy setting up our three locations around the building. The first was a concrete wall inside the youth room where I simply set a work light up against the wall to light up their pearly whites.

That was going to be the verse room. Then I went outside to a small grassy plot of land where I planned to have them dance around and just be eight-year-old girls.

Finally, the choruses would be filmed on the church stage where we had gathered lots of instruments for them to play as they were singing along. So simple. So quick. Probably only three takes a piece. And so perfect.

Fortunately, everything went off like a dream. There is no Carlos-type twist with things going wrong. The girls had a blast. Even if I hadn't been there to film a music video, they would have had a blast just playing.

The next day I spent six hours editing this future MTV Music Video Award winner. I put it on YouTube, emailed the parents, and bang—their kids were stars. I still remember some of the text messages I got from dads and moms that night. Confessing they were teary, they shared, "Thank you for giving my child this gift."

That was the best part about this whole production—I set out to make a moment for my daughter (granted, it was a way-over-the-top moment), but in the midst of making something beautiful for her, I ended up spreading the beauty to everyone.

This video was the talk of the girls in the children's ministry for a while. And honestly, it's a really bad video. But my daughters and their friends felt special, and that is really where Moment Making comes in. The essence of it was giving the girls a stage where they could have their moment in the spotlight.

* * *

When someone feels the true worth of who they are because you stopped what you were doing and made life about them, you have hit on an essential component of Moment Making.

Can't you see that truth in the very presence and being of Jesus? Look at Matthew 20:28: "Just as the Son of Man did not come to be served, but to serve, and to give his life as a ransom for many."

We all know that Jesus served everyone he encountered. He was all about making the moments with them about *them* — showing them they were loved, that they were valued by their Father in heaven. But think about it. It wasn't just in what he did while he was here that we see him making moments for us. The fact that he came and hung out with us at all is a monumental moment in the history of humanity.

Jesus came to do something incredibly special for us. He came to make sure we knew our worth, our value to God. He pulled out all the stops to show us that we matter. He literally came from heaven to earth! I'm no theologian — but this is pretty massive, right?

If you bought a ticket and flew across the country to see me, I think I'd be blown away. But Jesus? He's like, "Hey, I'm gonna come down from heaven for thirty-some-odd years. How's that for love?"

So, as you start looking for ways to make the people in your life feel special, remember the key: It's not about just making a moment that stands out and is spectacular. It's about making someone feel valued *through* that moment. Because of the thought you put into it. Because they know they are worth that much.

Fourteen little girls with passion and imagination plus one balding, slightly overweight dad, armed with a makeshift crew, came together to make a magical moment in which those girls lived out a dream.

I know Seanna loved it. I hope it's a memory that will last a lifetime. And who knows, maybe a moment that will give her the first line of that chorus ... "Someday I'll be living in a big ol' city ..."

CHAPTER 2

CREATING HOPE

The south-facing wall of the Crema Café overlooks the river charging along the east bank of downtown Nashville. The wall is floor-to-ceiling glass. I love café windows. I'm a hopeless romantic, and I love seeing the separation between my reality and what's outside. You can see the Titans Stadium on the other side of the river, and when the sky is its perfect Atlantic blue ... well, Norman Rockwell may as well go ahead and paint a picture of you against that glass. It's that perfect.

Another reason I love to sit by that window is that every single person who walks in has to walk past me. They all are subject to my gaze. Okay, maybe it's judgment. Not so much judging their spirit or soul, but whether they are going to fit into the hipster crowd in the coffee shop. I'm on the edge. Actually over the edge. My jeans aren't skinny enough and my receding hairline recedes a bit too far. So I go the opposite direction and try to shock the hipsters with Jay-Z meets East Nash. It works. At least the shocking part.

A year or so ago, as I was sitting on my east-window perch, I saw someone walk in that definitely did not fit the mold. She was about 6'6", in some killer heels, legs that stretched the length of the Mississippi, and swag that would swallow you whole. This person either just got off the plane from Vegas or was on her way to Vegas 'cause there's no way that she lived in my town, Nashville, Tennessee.

I watched, as I do, and saw her order coffee. After she dropped her bills on the counter and paid for her caffeine, she turned around and gave a glare that would make Medusa freeze. The pace at which she swung her head and surveyed the room was astounding. Superhero-like. I'm assuming that she caught and mentally destroyed around seven or eight people before they had the chance to look away. She looked good doing it. Like she does this all the time.

"Nicole. Your order's ready!" the barista yelled.

"Thanks, babe," Nicole responded.

Hold on. That voice. That voice was not the voice of a 6'6" model named Nicole. That voice was the voice of a 6'7" model named Chuck. Nicole took her coffee and her bag to the corner table and pulled out a phone.

By this point I was *all* up in her business. I knew Nicole was not an everyday female. I knew Nicole had a story. I knew I needed to know her story. I knew a moment was calling. Created Moment? Received Moment? Rescued Moment? I wasn't sure. But one was there, and I was taking it. So I seized the opportunity, quickly packed up my bag, and started walking her way. There was a seat at her table, and I straight-up took it.

"Um. Excuse me? This seat is taken," she said without even taking her eyes off her phone.

"By who?" I asked.

"Not by you," she replied.

But in her reply I saw a smirk. Understand it was only about 10 percent smirk, but it was the look that told me there was something inside of her that was open to me to sit there.

"Okay, game's over. I walked over here for a reason. I'm not quite sure what it is, but I'm here now. So if you really are working or have some important stuff to get done, I'll leave. But if you don't, I have a question."

"You a reporter or something?" Nicole asked.

"Or something," I replied.

"Look. I'm not a hooker. So if you want ..."

"What's it like," I asked, "to be you? To be Nicole? To order coffee?... To go to work?... To crush people with a single look and snap of the neck?"

For this I earned a giggle.

"Boyfriend, you ain't got the time in your day nor the space in your dome for the answer to that question," she replied, only this time, lifting her eyes completely off of her phone and finally locking eyes with me.

"Try me," I replied.

The next two hours were brought to you by authenticity, fear, pain, sorrow, with a seasoning of joy sprinkled on top just to make life bearable. Nicole actually did live in Nashville. And Nicole hadn't always been Nicole. I learned a lot about what it means to be a transgender that day. I learned that transgender doesn't actually mean transsexual. I learned that transgender doesn't mean cross-dressing. I also learned how to put my money where my mouth is.

"Me and some girlfriends are going honky-tonkin' tonight."

"Is that an invitation?" I asked.

"Not so much an invitation. I guess more of a thank-you. It's our way of showing you what real fun looks like."

I'd thought I made my moment. I got up. I'd walked across the room. I'd made conversation. But little did I know there was more to come.

"Okay. I'll be there."

Seven hours later I found myself standing on the corner of Broadway and Fifth. Music and beer pouring out of every door on the block. This was Nashville. More talent on the stages on that street than most cities have all together. And all they were getting paid was twenty-five dollars and free beer. This city is a trip.

Nicole had texted me that she and her friends were running late. So there I was, standing outside The Stage, a thirty-six-year-old married father of three waiting for my transgender friends. Their delayed arrival, however, didn't mean there was no party going on. I'd assume from the accent of the twelve or so drunk camo-wearing patrons who'd just stumbled out the door that they lived at least forty-five miles outside the city limits and were in town for a good time. But all I kept thinking as I watched the C-List version of the *Duck Dynasty* cast was ... *Nicole wants to party with these guys?*

When the cab rolled up and the door opened, it was like the opening scene of *Oceans 11*. Only the transgender version. Actually, maybe it was *Oceans 12*, but you get the idea: slo-mo, guns drawn, action about to occur. I swear I was watching a movie. They filed out at about sixty frames per second, legs emerging first.

Leading the group was the short one. This girl was 5'2" with arms bigger than the Hulk's. She wore a blue dress and blue heels. The next one out had the little black dress on and literally leaped out of the van, landing right next to me and saying, "You must be Carl."

"Car*los*," I replied, annoyed.

"Yea, whatever."

Finally, the ringleader appeared. Nicole rolled out with arms in the air, not unlike an NBA player who had just completed an aerial assault on an opposing player and was walking back down the court with arms raised in victory.

"What? *What?*" she cried.

I realized what was happening. Nicole and her friends had come down to Broadway not to party, but to fight ... ready to brawl, knowing that the world was against them and with chips on their shoulders. Within ten seconds one of the necks that was red launched a verbal assault that made my virgin, church-staff ears melt. Oh, the horror!

Again, in slow motion (because everything looks better that way) Nicole turned around and headed toward this little guy. She outweighed him by at least seventy-five pounds. He was about to lose—and in a big way. I stood there ... knowing that inside Nicole was someone dying to be loved. Pushing ensued ...

"Hey! *Hey!!* He's not worth it. You're worth more than that ...," I screamed.

Nothing. No response. By this point her two wing ladies were on their way and loosening their heels.

"*Nicole!* C'mon. Just look at me!"

She turned. She looked. And I was obviously messing up her game plan.

"*What!*" she yelled.

"You are worth so much more than this. Let's go inside and have some fun. C'mon."

The verbal assault from the Dukes of Hazzard boys wasn't slowing, and it took everything in the power of Carlos's Angels to back down. Carlos's Angels. They didn't even know I had claimed them as my girls, but I was going with it.

To my surprise Nicole actually stopped. She walked over to me and put one hand on each cheek. I looked up into her eyes—up because she was almost a foot taller than I.

"Carlitos ... no one has told me I'm worth anything, ever. Who are you really, Mr. Carrrrrrrlos?" Nicole asked with a smirk on her face.

"I'm Nicole's friend. And probably that guy's guardian angel, 'cause, let's be honest—you were about to kick that guy's—," I explained.

More laughter. I turned toward the almost-victim of Nicole's fists and yelled, "Hey, Cleetus. You're welcome!" to which I can

33

only assume he was invisibly more grateful than he could admit at that moment.

"This is Claire and this is J-Lo," she introduced. "We call her J-Lo 'cause, c'mon, just look at that booty."

"Hey J-Lo and Claire. I'm Carlos. Wanna dance?"

We piled into the StageCoach, and they made a beeline toward the middle of the dance floor. They were ready to party. I was not. My heart was heavy. It was heavy all night. I mean, listen, you can't keep Carlitos off the dance floor. And I danced till my feet hurt. But watching Carlos's Angels all night and watching the dance floor empty like someone just stepped on an anthill when they walked on was heartbreaking. It was breaking knowing that there are truly people like my new friends in this world who will almost *never* find community outside of each other.

All I kept thinking as I watched people part like the Red Sea as they walked by was how I pray if and when I get "Nicole" to my church or to your church, that the crowd would not part like the Red Sea but overwhelm them with waves of love.

The night came to a close, and instead of Nicole and her friends hailing another cab, I offered to take them home. I drove about ten miles south of Nashville and dropped them off at Nicole's place.

"No one talks to me like you do. Not even my friends. It's like you hope for me," she texted me later that night.

I hope for her? What does that even mean? Then I walked to the bathroom to wash my face. I looked in the mirror and said this out loud: "I hope for her. I hope for her." And when I said it out loud, I completely knew what she meant. She meant the same thing we all mean. She wants the same thing we all want. For someone to desire that we get the best in life. For someone to put themselves and their desires aside for a moment and place all their hope on us. I want that too, Nicole. We all do.

I'd love to end this story with "Nicole and I are now best friends. We text daily, and she feels the love on a consistent basis." But that's not the truth. Nicole hasn't answered my texts. She didn't return my calls. And I stopped texting and calling.

* * *

See, sometimes moments are made for just that ... a moment. You and I are not the saviors of this world. There is someone who already pulls that off much better than we could even hope to. He also pulls off this Moment-Making thing much better than us.

Take for example John 8:3–6. It's that lady we whisper about. Let's name her Nicole. Jesus dropped a Moment-Making gem on her and her accusers:

> The teachers of the law and the Pharisees brought in a woman caught in adultery. They made her stand before the group and said to Jesus, "Teacher, this woman was caught in the act of adultery. In the Law Moses commanded us to stone such women. Now what do you say?" They were using this question as a trap, in order to have a basis for accusing him.

Now here is where we can learn from the Moment-Making master. Jesus didn't launch into a tirade defending this woman. Jesus didn't tell these guys to take a hike. You know what he did? Jesus got dirty. He bent down and started drawing something in the sand.

There are countless theories as to what he drew. We will never know. But you know what we do know? We know that he did not immediately launch into verbal war with these guys. We know that he paused.

Pausing. Such an important part of Moment Making. When we forget to pause we don't make room for things to catch up with us. We can't let the best ideas rise to the surface.

Inside pause we find tension release. Inside pause we find serenity. I think Jesus paused to bring all of this out. I think he may have just drawn a smiley face in the sand. Maybe tic-tac-toe. Who knows? But we do know that he paused and made everyone wait.

Then he said, "Let any one of you who is without sin be the first to throw a stone at her" (John 8:7). Again he stooped down and wrote on the ground. He unpaused for what had to take no longer than three seconds, then paused again ... and back to drawing in the dirt.

I can only imagine the people watching. The Pharisees were mortified, and those whom he was teaching were probably marveling. The purposefulness of this moment cannot be lost. There was intent behind his pause. And in this he let the Pharisees, slowly but surely, leave one by one until only the woman was left. Their exchange went like this:

> Jesus straightened up and asked her, "Woman, where are they? Has no one condemned you?"
>
> "No one, sir," she said.
>
> "Then neither do I condemn you," Jesus declared. "Go now and leave your life of sin." (John 8:10–11)

I don't know what was more powerful, the fact that Jesus had scattered the Pharisees with his question or the fact that he didn't drop a sermon on this woman. He simply showed love and forgiveness.

I think as we launch into this life of making moments we need to take an example from this man called Jesus. We should pause and make sure that the next thing we say, in any moment, is worthy of saying it.

We need to make sure that we don't overshare and that we simply show love. This is a monumental concept. To make sure that a moment of chaos is wrapped in a moment of peace. And out of that peace we will find that our moments can truly redeem people's hope in themselves.

I asked Nicole to pause instead of reacting to the hatred with violence. I asked her to give herself a chance to be more. And in that pause, I believe she found some glimmer of hope.

CHAPTER 3

CREATING JOY

Heather and I were destined to be together. But I will admit, even on the day that we said "I do," we had no idea what that meant. I mean, seriously, who really does?

We often sit back and laugh over how naive we were and how we knew *absolutely nothing* about each other. I mean I knew that I liked the way her smile would turn crooked sometimes. It made butterflies fill my heart, and they would make their way into the back of my throat. I now know that it turns crooked when she wants me to stare a little bit longer. And so I stare a little bit longer.

I also knew I loved that she knew every word to every song on every Garth Brooks album. I didn't know, however, that she cries every single time "The Dance" is played. Every single time.

Sometimes I'll hold my iPod to her ear while she is sleeping and hit play so that she can wake up full of emotion. Actually, I've never done that. But it's such a great idea.

Our puppy love has grown into outright, full-grown-Labrador sloppy love. Although I'm not sure why they call it puppy love, I have a feeling it has something to do with what happens when you first see a puppy. Adoration replaces all good decision-making processes. Most people who see a puppy have no need for a puppy but take the puppy home anyway. They can't see past the clumsy cute love. Not until the yelping begins at 3:30 a.m. That is the point when love truly begins — when you make the decision *to love* as opposed to just *feeling* love.

I think I give my bride more 3:30 a.m. moments than anyone on the planet deserves. Still, she keeps waking up and comforting me in spite of my inability to grow up. And I think it's because she's in love with my Moment Making.

You see, I'm addicted to creating moments. I am addicted. And I'd go out on a limb to say that more than 99 percent of these moments succeed not necessarily because the moment itself was a success, but because attempting to create a moment for someone is sometimes the only moment they need.

They need you to care enough to try. It is in this that we find the beauty of creating moments. The moment, in the end, is often not the one we set out to create in the first place. But that's okay.

The truth is that even when the plan fails ... well, at least you planned it in the first place. It's where the phrase "It's the thought that counts" comes from. But the thought shouldn't count unless there is an action that follows even if that action fails. You acted. And actions are the legs to thoughts.

2007

Wife. Three kids. New tract home in Southern California. Ten years at the same job. Great friends. Then one day ...

"Hey, babe. I think we need to move to Atlanta."

And off we went.

This certainly was not an easy decision for us. I mean, I'd been leading worship at Sandals Church for ten years. Starting when I was twenty-two years young. We got married there. Had all our babies while we were there. But then came an opportunity to take that Sharpie we had been writing our story with and change the color.

Northpoint Community Ministries had contacted me about joining the leadership team at their Buckhead Church campus and running their weekend experiences.

I was sure my SoCal wife would *never* go for the idea. So I mentioned it in a nonchalant way while we were talking about what to make for dinner. "That sounds miserable," she said. "Not Atlanta. Not leaving here."

Two weeks later she walked downstairs after doing her Bible study and said those words that changed the trajectory of our Moment-Making journey ... just as her role as Director/Producer would dictate, "Hey, babe. I think we need to move to Atlanta." Four weeks later I was there.

Everything about the South was a shock for my poor family. I mean, the job was going well, the house was great, and the white picket fence was a nice touch. But I had snatched my wife out of the only community she had known as a Christian and replaced it with the South. (Even if she was the one who actually "heard from God" about us moving.) I knew something had to be done.

Heather's birthday was coming up, and if I knew one thing, it was that her best friend, Jacinda, would make all things right in the world. Women BFFs are different than male BFFs. Guys don't find kinship in having our wives pregnant together. Guys don't find kinship in going to the restroom together. Guys don't find kinship in two-hour phone conversations. But our wives do.

Jacinda and Heather talk every ... single ... day. I talk to my best friend maybe once a week. *Maybe.* But these two were inseparable. And thus began the plot to surprise Heather with a visit from her best friend. There were a few details that stood in the way. The first of which was the three thousand miles that separated them. It was gonna take some cash to get her to Atlanta. I had a credit card and went ahead and committed the Dave Ramsey crime. Okay. That was easy. Flight was booked. We just had to pay it off for a few weeks.

Here's the next problem. Jacinda can't lie. She just can't. I, on the other hand, could do anything to pull off creating a great moment ... even cold-hearted deceit. So I warned her, "Jacinda, listen. You *can't* let her find out. I mean you can't even smile while you guys are on the phone because I know she will hear that smile three thousand miles away."

My wife can break you. She breathes discernment like I breathe air. But through all the conversations, through all the *daily* phone calls, Jacinda was certain that Heather didn't know. And for this I was grateful.

The night before Jacinda flew out we had one final strategy session. The plan was that I would act like I was going to work but would drive to the airport instead to get her. I would then take her to work with me until it was time to go home. Then I would drop Jacinda off half a block away from the house, and she would wait until I texted her; then she would sneak up the side of the house, through the back gate, and into the back door. I would have to find a way to distract Heather while she made her way up the drive- way. The front of our house was completely covered with windows overlooking the street, so she *had* to wait for my text.

While we were driving back to the house from my office, Jacin- da's phone rang. It was Heather.

"Answer it. Just play it cool," I said.

So Jacinda answered and was the most amazing con artist on the planet for about twenty-five seconds. She was flawless.

"How'd I do?" she asked.

"Brilliant," I replied, "except for the part where you said it's Tuesday ... 'cause it's Wednesday."

We drove into my neighborhood and I dropped her off in the bushes. No, really, I did.

"You ready?" I asked.

She nodded her head.

I left her there, drove up the driveway, took a deep breath, and walked in.

"Hey, family! Daddy's home!"

There is one thing that Heather tells me I do to give away a surprise every single time. She says I overdo it. I can't help it. It's like I was born to be an actor on a Univision novella. I overact everything. *Stop overdoing it, man. Just relax*, I reminded myself.

Within a few seconds I was greeted by the entire family. I could tell by the look on Heather's face that she was onto me. I didn't know how. I just knew she was. And I had to fix it.

"Is everything okay, baby?"

There I go again. Over-the-top questions to anyone I may think is suspicious.

"Umm. Yeah. Why are *you* acting so weird?" she replied.

"Oh, it was just a heck of a day. Sorry."

So I followed her to the kitchen where she was busy making dinner. She wasn't supposed to make dinner for another hour.

"Uh. Why are you making dinner? Umm. I mean. Why are you making dinner so early?" I asked.

"Why does it matter? Why are you being so weird? The kids are hungry. You can have dinner later if you want. But we're hungry."

Oh baby. This was going south fast. I peeked out the front window and could see Crouching Tiger Hidden Jacinda in the bushes by the mailbox. She was doing her job. I was failing at mine. I needed to get Heather upstairs, and since she was already onto me, I knew I couldn't lie.

I could not lie about why I needed her upstairs. I couldn't say I needed her help finding a boot in my closet. I couldn't say I needed her help cleaning the ceiling fan. I couldn't say I needed her to help me make the bed.

These are all things I never do, and to do that right then would be surprise suicide. So I did what any God-fearing, family-loving man would do ... I took one for the team.

"Okay. You busted me, babe. I don't know what it is. I honestly don't know what it is today. Maybe it's your hair. Maybe it's your outfit. Maybe it's the way your voice sounded on the phone earlier, but I can't handle it. I can't wait till tonight. I need you right now."

"Daddy. You can't have her. We're hungry," sounded off a little Whitt a few feet behind me.

"Babe. Can you wait thirty minutes? It won't take long to cook dinner. Then we can put a movie on for the kids."

Can we take a station break to extol the gift that is Netflix? Allowing parents to make love while the children are awake since 2002.

"I can't wait, baby. I need you now," I replied.

"*Ugh*. Okay. Kids. Go pick out a movie. Mommy and Daddy are gonna go have special time."

On the way upstairs I pulled out the phone and texted Jacinda: "The eagle has landed." I thought it was cool.

"You have to get one more fix of social media before we have special time?" I heard from behind me.

"Oh, no, baby. Just turning my phone on silent."

We went in the bedroom and shut the door. And I was praying Jacinda was on her way in. What went on behind that closed door is for another book altogether, but I will say this: Jacinda was wondering why she was sitting alone in the living room for so long.

Hours ... (cough) ... minutes later we walked downstairs and the surprise was revealed. Tears were flowing and laughter was sounding when Jacinda, being emotionally and spiritually connected to Heather in ways I still don't understand, stood straight up and said: "Wait a second! Did you guys just ...?" And so began four days of BFF time for my wife and Jacinda.

As I sit on a tour bus reflecting on that day, I have a smile as bright as the noon sky. Why? Because the process of creating the moment was, for me, more exciting than the moment itself. It's often that way.

Moments are the exclamation points to the sentences. An exclamation point without a sentence is useless. It takes the sentence to bring meaning to the exclamation point. See?

!

* * *

So as you are creating moments, don't take the process for granted. Don't let the moment happen without realizing that the intention that comes before the moment is what makes it all meaningful.

We see a great illustration of this in Luke chapter 10 when Jesus visits with Mary and Martha in Bethany. I'm sure you remember the comparison of the sisters, one who was busy cooking and cleaning and preparing, and the other who sat listening.

In their story we find Jesus and his disciples walking down a road, exhausted, I'm sure. I have to drive to Atlanta once a week from Nashville and *that* exhausts me. So to know that Jesus was walking *every* day means that he totally appreciated an open door and a place to rest his feet. As they were walking, they came across a woman named Martha. Martha, in typical south Georgia fashion, opened her door to Jesus and his disciples and, in typical Southern fashion, went straight to the kitchen to begin cooking and cleaning and doing all that busywork. Her sister, Mary, on the other hand, did the exact *opposite*.

I call this pulling a Sohaila. Whenever it's time to clean our house, we often find Sohaila, minutes after we've all started, sitting in a corner with our cat, Riggins, having a fantastic conversation.

I know how frustrating it is to live with that person. I live with her! So I can empathize with Martha as she walked out of the kitchen and straight up to Jesus and said, "Lord, don't you care that my sister has left me to do the work by myself? Tell her to help me!"

Jesus's response to her was pretty clear: He simply stated, "Martha, Martha, you are worried and upset about many things, but few things are needed — or indeed only one. Mary has chosen what is better, and it will not be taken away from her" (Luke 10:41–42).

Drop the mic. Walk off the stage. Jesus just dropped a truth in two sentences that changed the Moment-Making process for us all. See, the party they were throwing for Jesus was the exclamation point. His visit was a very special moment for those who had the chance to meet him. But the story that comes before it is partly in the preparations Martha was making, but *mostly* in the conversation Mary was having. That busyness was just filler.

The real story, the sentence that comes before the exclamation point is what Mary was doing. She sat and listened. She spent time connecting with Jesus and getting to know him. She was learning that he didn't need to have four kinds of hors d'oeuvres, fresh linens in the bathroom, and a dusting job that would pass a white-glove test.

These things are fantastic and many of you reading this are really good at hosting people. But I always remind those gifted in hosting and event planning to make sure that you enjoy the party too. Spend time with those you are honoring with the party. Then they will appreciate the party that much more.

When I go into a church for the first time to lead worship, I try to stay out of the green room and in the lobby as much as possible. Why? Because although the exclamation point may be what happens on stage, the sentence before the exclamation point is most certainly what happens off stage.

I try to greet and hug as many people as possible. I go pew by pew and welcome people to church, even if I have never been to the church before! When they see me go on stage, they no longer see some guy trying to get them to sing songs. They now see the guy who just hugged them and welcomed them to church. They remember the sentence, and it makes the exclamation point that much stronger.

Jesus was the primo Moment Maker. He was better at it than we will ever be. He knew what made moments memorable. He knew what made moments valuable. He knew what made moments worth having.

Going back to what I said at the beginning of this chapter, it is important to *understand* that sometimes the moment is in the thought that went into planning it rather than the execution. Martha was all about trying to create a moment for Jesus by hosting him properly, while Mary was demonstrating the thought behind it. They both were trying to honor Jesus, but Mary was actually getting the connection and Martha was missing the point.

That isn't to say we don't need Marthas. Without their attention to detail we might throw a party and forget the food ... or forget to book the plane ticket ... or forget to come up with a good plan B if plan A goes awry. But we can't get so caught up in the execution that we forget about the experience.

So as you become Moment Makers, as you look toward the moments that will serve as exclamation points in your lives, don't forget to enjoy writing the sentence that goes before the exclamation point. For an exclamation point alone is nothing without the sentence that goes before it. Write, my friends. Write the sentence. And enjoy the moment you get to finish that sentence with a downward stroke and a dot.

!

CHAPTER 4

CREATING PERSPECTIVE

For centuries, Moment-Making men have been called "hopeless romantics." Hopeless. Without hope. But if the movie industry is any indicator, the world seems to love these men who will stop at nothing to prove their love to the object of their desire.

Apparently, there are women out there in the world who love to be pursued in such a way—persistent, unrelenting, yearning . . . stalker-y?

The brutal, unflattering truth is this is what a hopeless romantic is, people.

Have you ever looked at a romantic comedy from a pragmatic point of view? Think about it. That guy who shows up outside your house and wakes your neighbors while he shouts at your window that he won't leave until you talk to him? Yeah. Without the Hollywood soundtrack he is restraining-order material.

I'm not sure about you, but I see how this could be a little frightening.

When I first kissed Jennifer Lee in seventh grade, we had decided that we were going to kiss for twenty minutes straight. All I know is that I looked like Bozo the clown the entire next week. My lips were chapped and red, and I knew at that point: too much of a good thing is never a good thing.

When I first tossed my toddler child up in the air so I could hear that tiny giggle and squeal come rising from the depths of her soul, I did what any good father would do. I tossed her higher. The giggle grew louder. So I tossed higher . . . The giggle turned to a squall, and I ended up with her breakfast on my face. Four feet was too high.

When I had my first bite of an In-N-Out burger, I knew the Lord had brought me there. I soon ordered four patties. Then five. Then late one night, around 2:00 a.m., I learned that six patties were too many. Even for a twenty-two-year-old fifth-year senior.

Too much of a good thing is not good. Even if that good thing is romance. Maybe *especially* if it is romance. Alas, I didn't have this wisdom in my dome back in 1990-something when I met Sarah Palmer. She was the kindest, sweetest, most soft-spoken girl at my college. She would never dream of saying anything that would hurt another person. We would Rollerblade around campus, and it was like a scene from a Bob Ross painting. Picturesque, serene, full of happy trees and a happy couple. I really liked Palmer.

I was a junior, she was a freshman, and I knew that I was created to spend every waking moment with her. So I did. And then a few weeks later, after the time of our lives and professing our undying love for each other, she sat me down and had this conversation with me:

"Hey. I think we should maybe scale back a little and maybe kinda just be friends for a bit," said Palmer.

My translation: She hates me. What does "maybe scale back a little and maybe kinda just be friends for a bit" even *mean*? I'll tell you what that meant . . .

It meant Carlos Enrique Whittaker was about to turn it on. And by turn it on, I mean I put a plan in motion to deliver to Palmer a birthday that only a "hopeless romantic" would devise. I would give her what forever would be remembered by the alumni of Berry College as "Happy Palmer Day."

Two weeks after the "scale back" talk I prepared all day and night for the birthday of her dreams. I worked in the School of Education and Human Sciences and had access to their copy machines. So I did what any normal hopeless romantic would do. I made about *one thousand eight hundred* fliers with her high-school senior picture on it and the words "HAPPY PALMER DAY" written across the top and bottom of the flier. Because what eighteen-year-old freshman in college *doesn't* want to have a close-up of their face plastered all over campus?

I stayed up all night long. Every car windshield. Every classroom door. Every stall in every bathroom. Every locker in every locker room. Every door in every dorm in every building. Every single person walking on that campus that day would see the love of my life.

Her favorite candy was Peeps. At least that's what I thought. So I bought at least one hundred boxes of Peeps and created a path from her dorm room door to the door of her cute little VW Convertible Rabbit in the parking lot. A *long* way away. When she got to her car, she would find it filled with flowers and more candy. And I planned for her to find letters all day long professing my undying love for her. She could not turn a corner without the world knowing it was her birthday.

This, my friends, was obviously what I thought "maybe scale back a little and maybe kinda just be friends for a bit" meant. Clearly, we just had different interpretations of that.

At dinner that night I remember my best friend Eric saying, "Sooo. Don't you think you went a bit overboard today?"

Without blinking I said, "Oh man, I've only just started."

I left the dining hall and proceeded to the mall to pick up about a hundred helium-filled balloons and her Mrs. Fields cookie cake with "Happy Palmer Day" scrawled across the face. It was my grand finale. It was the final inning where I was gonna hit that grand slam.

Earlier that day I had run into her and got an awkward side hug and a "thanks" from her. My plan was obviously working. Move over "scale it back," and hello "let's get married."

It was dark in her closet. I didn't know how long I was going to have to stand there. Sarah and her friend Jennifer had gone out for a run about thirty minutes earlier, and I had moved quickly in that short time to fill her dorm room with the helium balloons and place the cookie cake on her bed before she could come back. Then I hid, waiting for my big surprise moment. Minutes felt like hours, and I was practicing my speech in my head.

"Palmer. I know you wanted more space and stuff. But I know one thing: I love you. And I need you to be my girl. I'll go to the ends of the world to shout it. I'm in love with you!"

Keys shaking. Door handle turning. Door opening. Light switch clicking. My hand reaching for the closet door handle. My hand turning closet door handle. Jennifer speaking these words . . .

"Um . . . Sarah, what are you going to do? Are you going to tell him? He totally still thinks you like him. Did he not hear you when you said it was over?"

  . . .

  . . .

  . . .

  . . .

  . . .

Yeah. Those spaces are there so you can sit on that bad boy for a second.

I stood in that closet, world crumbling around me. I had a decision to make.

1. *I could ride it out.* I could ride out the excruciating pain of hearing the truth and wait for Jennifer to leave and hopefully Palmer to follow and then make my run for it.

2. *I could run.* I could barge out, hands up, weeping and screaming, "I'm sorry! I'm sorry! I didn't mean to hear all of that! I didn't mean to be in here and listen to everything you guys just said! I'm sorry! I'm an idiot! *WAAAAHHHHHH!*" and sprint down her hallway while she screamed "Carlos! Come back! Let's talk!"

I chose option #2.

She was fast. But I was faster. I jumped on my mountain bike and headed east from the St. Mary dormitory compound. Being on the largest college campus in America gave me one advantage in that moment: it was gonna be easy to hide.

I found a section of grass on the west side of the School of Education building and collapsed into a heaping mess of an emotionally charged twenty-year-old kid.

I'd made a mess by trying to make a moment when a moment wasn't needed. I lay there for what felt like hours. Only weeks before, Palmer and I had lain only yards away looking up at the stars and dreaming about the future.

I must have slept for at least forty-five minutes. When I opened my eyes I could feel the dried salt from my tears cracking on my skin. "'Los. C'mon, man. We've all been worried. Everyone's looking for you. Get up, bro. Shake it off. It'll be okay." Jeff was my RA. We walked our bikes all the way back to the dorms and talked the whole time about where I'd gone wrong and how I could have handled the situation better.

The moment Jennifer and Palmer walked in the room and reacted to my gesture, the reality of my situation became crystal clear. I knew I had failed. I had taken what should have been a small thought-out moment and turned it into a disaster of zeppelin-exploding proportion.

Palmer was as grace-filled and gentle as she could possibly be in the midst of her own humiliation. Talk about going out in a blaze of glory. It was obvious that I'd ruined my shot of ever dating a girl at my school again (until the new flock of freshmen came in).

But that day did a lot for me. As *crazy* as it was, it gave me great insight for my Moment-Making journey.

* * *

As you create moments, you must make sure they fit into the truth of your situation, into the shape of your reality. There is nothing worse than trying to get a too-small ring off your finger that you should have never forced on in the first place.

There is a time for big. There is a time for little. There is a time for in-between. Figuring out when to pull out the fireworks and when to stick with the Hallmark card may be a little more difficult than you'd assume, because as a famous poet (Shakespeare, I think) once said, "Love is blind."

When love motivates us, we have a tendency to become overwhelmed by those feelings, and we want to make sure everyone knows how we feel. Love is a feeling that is very hard to keep contained, and sometimes we don't know when to quit. At least I don't.

Think about how Jesus operated. There were times when he went big and there were times when he worked small. We know about the story of him feeding the multitude out of a little boy's lunch pail. That's huge. That's grandiose. But early in his ministry he also did a lot of healing when he told people not to tell anyone else how it happened.

In Matthew 9:29–30, after a few blind men had trailed him for quite a ways, even following him into a home where he was a guest, he touched their eyes and said, "According to your faith let it be done to you." And then poof! They could see.

It was a massive moment in the lives of these men, but Jesus asked them to keep it quiet. Actually, he warned them sternly. That is, not asking. So why did he do that? I'm sure there were reasons we won't understand this side of heaven, but I think it was because he had other stuff to do in that community and didn't want to draw attention to his posse. Fireworks ... small. It was still a firework for sure! Restoring sight! But Jesus made it more of a sparkler moment. Kinda like the kind you give your kids so they don't blow their limbs off on the Fourth of July.

In Mark 1 Jesus does this again. Not only with the instruction to keep it to themselves, but again with a *stern* command not to tell anyone. And in Mark 5, one of the most famous reports of Jesus and his miraculous ministry, Jesus brought a girl back to life and immediately told the astonished friends and family not to share their story. And again, it says he said it strongly. This time Scripture says he "gave strict orders not to let anyone know" (v. 43).

I would venture a guess and say Jesus asked them to keep quiet because he knew that if he turned into a one-man circus, he would not be able to go into any town after that without drawing a lot of attention. That would ruin his chances for the intimate, one-on-one encounters he knew were so important to meeting individual needs.

Jesus knew the importance of having a time and a place for everything. He knew that there would come a time in his ministry when he would need to reveal to the masses who he was and what he could do; but he also knew the moment that happened, his effectiveness would diminish.

He did come to save everyone, but in the beginning he focused on doing it one person at a time so the moment would be real for each person he touched; he knew exactly what was right for each person and for each encounter, and it wasn't always "bigger is better."

This is another example of where the pause is crucial. As we step into this lifestyle of Moment Making, we need to remember this step. Pausing is critical to discerning where you go with the moment you want to create.

When I'm in a creative meeting and we're going full-force, brainstorming an idea, I start to see that look in everyone's eyes —

you know the look. It's the same look I had when my buddy Eric tried to convince me this whole Happy Palmer Day was a bad idea. It's the look of being so in love with an idea that you start to lose focus on the goal. The purpose has the potential to be lost in the execution.

So when I see that look ... we pause. And by *pause* I mean completely stop the meeting. By *pause* I mean step away completely from the idea. If you do that, you will find that every single time you pause when creating a moment—every time—the moment becomes better than it would have been without the pause.

You see, my friends, the desire to do something great for someone else is awesome and should be encouraged, but take the time to think it through. There is definitely something to be said for being impulsive, but it can get you into trouble. For example, when my wife tells me that she wants to take the weekend and rest because she's exhausted, that is not an invitation to plan a surprise party and make her cook for fifteen friends. That is the time to take the kids out and give her a break. Maybe bring home dinner so she doesn't have to cook.

Seizing an opportunity has its place, but even in those moments, taking time to step back and make sure it is a moment worth having can make all the difference in the world for the outcome. Doing something that is thoughtful means being thoughtful about the impact your moment has on where the other person is.

Pausing. Resting. Seeing. For a moment of silence can sometimes speak the loudest of all.

CHAPTER 5

CREATING THANKFULNESS

It was late when I pulled in at the hotel. I grabbed my guitar, my backpack, and the box of CDs I brought to sell at the festival. The box still had 181 out of 200 CDs left. Yes, it was that kind of day.

The second I walked into the lobby I smelled that hotel smell. You know the one. It's a mix of chlorine from the pool down the hall and air freshener from the lobby along with something being cooked in the bar to the right. I welcomed the smell. For me it meant I was about two minutes and forty-seven seconds from feeling the cool of the backside of my pillow. And for this I was grateful.

The second thing I noticed was a group of soldiers standing around — mostly women. There were around twenty of them fresh off tour. Giggling. Talking on their cell phones. Looking like there could be no other place they'd rather be. I began to feel a small surge of pride invade my chest, enough to walk up to one of them and ask quite simply,

"Where you guys coming in from?"

"Eighteen miserable months in Afghanistan," one of the soldiers replied. "I get to see my baby tomorrow," she said.

Those thirteen words were full of emotion. Full of angst. Full of hope. Full of everything. Not happy nor sad. A little bit of both and lots in the middle. I felt some pressure over what to say next. People don't normally talk to me with that sort of intensity. She was staring straight into my eyes, almost in a doubtful way. Kinda like "this guy has no clue." And I didn't. So you know what I said?

"Well, thanks for doing that. I have no idea what that even looks like, but I'm pretty sure it makes what I do pale in comparison."

There was this unnaturally long pause. She knew what I was trying to say even though I butchered it. Right before I did more damage I heard the elevator go *ding*. I quickly turned, not waiting for a reply to my horrendous response and sprinted to the elevator.

I have this weird habit of standing at an elevator and waiting until the door is about to close before getting on, then I stick my hand in quickly and make it open back up. Maybe it's because I have a six-year-old who thinks it's magic. (I think it's magic too.) Well, I did it this time too, but it just slammed against my hand almost chopping it off.

I quietly laughed, while holding my throbbing hand, at my preschool compulsion that made me miss the elevator, but in no time flat it opened again. Barging out were six or seven rowdy male soldiers, obviously heading down the corridor toward the hotel bar. I wished I looked as happy as they did. "Please get off this elevator and let this lame excuse for a rock star go to sleep." I didn't actually say that, although I'm sure it was written all over my face.

You see, earlier that day I played on a stage in front of a crowd of forty thousand concertgoers. They weren't my fans, but they were real live people. And I sold nineteen CDs. Yea. Get me to bed. Room 618.

Pants off. SportsCenter on. Temperature set at 65. Down pillow. Cool comforter sprawled across my bag of bones. Perfect. I started thinking about the day and the bucket list item that was checked off my list: being a rock star. It is every guy's dream, and I became one. At least in theory. You see, I'm still the opening band. And you know what that means? I get up in front of forty thousand people and sing my heart out . . . while people check their phones, go buy cotton candy, and wait for the headliner to get on stage.

It's not a bad gig. I get to act like the rock star, but I'm really not. I am the band nobody knows but has to hear before they get to the ones they are really there to see.

Then I started to feel some connection to that ragamuffin crew of soldiers downstairs. They work hard for no glory. My mind began to race — "No. Stop it. No. Please. Just go to sleep, Carlitos."

Suddenly this thought flooded my dome. It was the kind of idea that you know wasn't coming from you. I literally plugged my ears and shouted, *"No, please!"*

Alas, it was futile. I needed to go back downstairs to the bar. I needed to know more about these guys and gals and try to tell them again how appreciative I was. Thirty-five seconds later I was back in my sweaty outfit from that afternoon and headed down to the bar.

The Lazy Lion Bar and Grill looked exactly as you'd imagine. Dark, a bit damp, and the bartender probably slept at the hotel. The entire place was empty except for the space right in front of the bar. The platoon of soldiers had morphed from the initial fifteen or so I met in the lobby to about forty. Some were fresh and out of their fatigues, some not. I considered just sitting back at a bar table and watching them celebrate from afar. Then I remembered that I am Carlos Whittaker — and I can't *not* join the party.

So I walked, slowly at first. Scoping out the soldiers to determine which ones looked like they would allow this tattooed guy with skinny jeans and a tank top to squeeze between them. There was one stool. Right between two soldiers. I awkwardly squeezed in. They both looked at me like, *Really?* I looked back like, *Yup.*

"Where's home?" I asked.

"California." The guy's name was Sam. "I haven't seen my babies in eighteen months. I can't wait."

Sam went on to answer every question I asked. *What kind of bed did you sleep on? Were you scared? Did you shoot anybody? Who did you miss the most? Did you ever get in trouble? Did they have Frosted Flakes?* On the other side of me Rachel chimed in.

"Did you know that we didn't have one drink the whole time we were there? Since I don't have any kids, this mojito is like my kid I couldn't wait to see."

We laughed and chatted for the better part of an hour. After a while, an older guy, who I assume was the leader dude (I'm military ignorant), stood up, cleared his throat, and lifted his glass.

"Ladies and gentlemen, I just want to thank you for serving your country. It has been my honor to serve alongside you this past year and a half, and I'd do it again if ever asked. I love you guys that much. You are heroes! Hear! Hear!"

"Hear! Hear!" they all shouted back . . . and so did I.

Yes, I was right along with them. There was an energy in the moment. There was a chill to the moment. Something strange was stirring inside me as his little speech was delivered.

I was smack-dab in the middle of a group of soldiers who had been on the other side of the world doing things I will never know, much less, understand. And earlier tonight I was moaning and complaining about being too hot as I got to sing in front of forty thousand people.

I don't remember much of the next three seconds. As soon as the cheering stopped for the captain, sergeant, ring-leader, old guy with swag, it happened. I don't know how. I don't know why. I didn't even feel my butt rising off my barstool.

"Attention! Hello! Over here!"

I found myself standing on the lower rung of my barstool. Forty-plus soldiers staring me straight in the face. Dead silent. I don't remember exactly what I said. But it was something to this effect:

"Listen, friends. You don't know me. I don't know you. I just spent an hour talking with Sam and Rachel about what your lives were like over the past eighteen months. I have no idea how hard it was for you. So I don't even think a *thank-you* would be adequate. But I do know one thing. Today I spent the day singing songs with my band in front of forty thousand people. We were singing about God. And it was good.

"I don't know what God you believe in. I don't know if you even believe in a god. But I do know this: I was able to sing to my God today because of what you are doing. I have the freedom to stand on a stage and tell the world that I love my God. And this is because you guys left your homes, families, friends, and comforts so that I could have mine.

"So, since I stood on a stage today pronouncing love for my God, I stand on this stage right now, before you, pronouncing my love and honor and respect to you. So, thank you, thank you from the bottom of this singer's heart. You move me to be a better man. God bless you guys."

My little *Braveheart* speech felt as though it lasted a lifetime. It was probably over in fifteen seconds. But the second I finished, at the end of my mess of a speech, the room filled with hoots, hollers, cheers, and some chant I could not join in on because I am not in that club.

"Hear! Hear!" I screamed.

"Hear! Hear!" they all screamed back.

"Hhheeeaaaarrr! Hhheeeaaaarrr!" I screamed louder.

"Hhhheeeeaaaarrrr! Hhhheeeeaaaarrrr!" They screamed louder.

It was amazing.

We were all high-five giving in this already epic moment when Moment Part Two decided to rise out of me ... "Oh, hey! Listen up! One more thing!"

Silence ... "The next round is on me!"

Explosions in the sky. You might as well have played the credits sequence for *Star Wars* in that moment. It was that epic. Drinks flowed. Laughter billowed. Hugs were passed around. I never thought once about the bill. I had $200 in cash in my wallet from some CDs I sold. As the night slowed down the bartender handed me my tab. One hundred and ninety-six bucks.

He looked at me and said:

"They could have made you a broke man tonight … but they all, every single one, asked what the most inexpensive beer was, and they ordered that one. They received your act of class with an act of class themselves."

The bartender, who I am halfway convinced was some form of Yoda reincarnated for just that moment, was right. They one-upped me because that is who they are.

As I was walking to the elevator, Rachel came running up to me. "No one remembers us. We feel forgotten. Thank you for not forgetting us. Thanks for sitting with us. We are you. You are us. Thank you."

* * *

I don't know why, but my mind raced to Luke 24. Jesus had just been crucified. He had been taken from his closest of friends. They were devastated. They were sad. They needed nothing more than comfort in that moment. Two of Jesus's disciples were on the road back home. Jesus had already beaten the grave. He had risen. Yet none of the disciples had seen this with their own eyes. They were relying on the account from some women who had been at the tomb. And then Jesus, the chief Moment Maker of all time, decides it's time for a moment.

In that account you find two of Jesus's disciples. We don't know much about them, but we do know they belonged to the band of brotherhood that began with Jesus. They were walking. Alone. Just the two of them when, from behind, a stranger appeared. They were probably so involved in their conversation of all that had transpired over the last few days that they did little to notice the stranger. I can imagine after the few days they had had, they weren't too excited about some random guy walking up and interrupting their time. I mean the last thing I want to have happen to me as I'm deep in convo with a friend is for some random guy to interrupt and want in. But this stranger was no ordinary stranger. This stranger was the Son of Man himself. Jesus Christ.

"What are you talking about?" he asked.

Scripture then tells us something interesting. It says that one of them replied to Jesus. But it gives us one more clue as to how they were feeling. It says that their faces were downcast. *Downcast.*

I can put on a happy face if I need to. And I sure as heck would have put on that face to get this guy off my back. But nope. Not these two. They were devastated and didn't care who knew. Then Cleopas answered just like any good, sad, and callous man would to such an intrusion. With sarcasm.

"Are you the only one visiting Jerusalem who does not know the things that have happened there in these days?"

Answering a question with a question. A sure fire way of getting rid of a little of that pent-up frustration. He dropped sarcasm on the King of Kings! But it's not over yet because Jesus then turns up the act.

"What things?" Jesus responded.

What things? *What things!* This is brilliant. I love Jesus even more after that comment. I'll take your dose of sarcasm and raise it $500.

"About Jesus of Nazareth," they replied. "He was a prophet, powerful in word and deed before God and all the people. The chief priests and our rulers handed him over to be sentenced to death, and they crucified him; but we had hoped that he was the one who was going to redeem Israel. And what is more, it is the third day since all this took place. In addition, some of our women amazed us. They went to the tomb early this morning but didn't find his body. They came and told us that they had seen a vision of angels, who said he was alive. Then some of our companions went to the tomb and found it just as the women had said, but they did not see Jesus." (Luke 24:19–24)

The two disciples pretty much spill it all. I'm sure they figure that this poor man can't go on without knowing the most important news of the day. There was no such thing as tweets trending to keep up with current affairs back then.

The next part of the story though, may be on my Top Ten Jesus Moment-Making Stories of All Time. When they got to their destination, Jesus didn't stop with them. He kept going. Knowing full well that they would invite him, he kept going because he wanted *them* to make the moment. He wanted them to experience healing by serving.

"Stay with us, for it is nearly evening; the day is almost over." And so he stayed.

When they got him to their pad, he sat at the table with them, took bread, gave thanks, broke it, and began to give it to them. He started into a long speech about prophets and the way things should be and then after a little bit of Scripture says, "Then their eyes were opened and they recognized him, and he disappeared from their sight" (Luke 24:30).

Oh, the glory. Oh, the realization. Oh, the joy.

Let's stop here for a second. I don't know about you, but if some of my best friends in the world were walking along a road, stricken with grief about my death, and I was actually alive, I would scream! *"Hey, guys! It's me! Los! Don't freak out! Relax! I'm alive!"*

But not Jesus. He actually disguised himself. You read that correctly. He made sure they could not recognize him. Why did he do this? I think it's because they would have wanted to cling to him, and he knew he couldn't stay. I also think he understood that they needed a way to process their pain and come to terms with why he had to leave them. They needed something else to focus on, such as this stranger, so they could begin to have some perspective.

Jesus's disciples stopped, stepped outside their own needs, and met the needs of another. By not sending this traveler on down the road, they opened themselves up to a moment. These friends of Jesus did a solid for a traveler by offering him a meal and a little rest from the road. As a bonus, they got an unexpected and much-needed moment with their Lord.

What happened with my friends in the bar turned out to be this same kind of double blessing. As I tried to give these returning soldiers a moment—to bless them—they gave me one. I was showing my gratitude to these men and women who had served me without knowing me, and in the middle of that they began to share with me—a total stranger—the abandonment they felt as they returned. My little gesture made them feel seen. They were acknowledged. Not passed over. Not just sent on their way down the road.

You know, as I think back on the encounter with my military friends I shudder at the thought of possibly missing that moment. This moment that was only available to me because I listened to that voice that was saying: "There is a moment waiting for you. A moment that can only happen in a setting of 'together.'" When Rachel thanked me ... well, the residue of that moment is still on me today.

Leaving Rachel, I got on the elevator, pressed the button, prayed the elevator door would shut so I could be alone, then cried all the way up six floors. I couldn't afford that round of drinks, but I also felt I couldn't afford not to buy it for them. It was a Top Five Life Moment for me.

I had what I thought was a moment earlier that day. You know that moment you dream about your whole life? That moment you think will define who you are. The moment where I stood in front of forty thousand people and had them sing with me as I led them in song. That one. Well, my bucket-list moment in front of forty thousand people paled in comparison to the moment in that bar in front of forty.

You see, it's not the size of "together" that counts. Being a Moment Maker is about way more than checking off your bucket-list items. The experiences on your list should mean something. It isn't about just doing fun, daring, or forbidden things. It is about *living*. The experiences you have, the moments you create, should leave a mark on the world and you. They should change everyone who is touched by them for the better.

So, as you make out your lists, fill them with moments that will make the life you have lived worth living and worth remembering. You may just find yourself slowly rising on a barstool and inviting a round of blessings into your own life.

PART TWO

RECEIVED MOMENTS

I always try to board first. Always. I'm a window guy, not an aisle guy, and I hate having to ask someone to stand up to let me in. Southwest Airlines is my worst enemy because they don't assign seats and force the entire plane full of passengers into accepting that the last forty people on the plane are 100% going to be stuck asking for the middle seat. Who wants to be a middle-seat asker?

This airline is a nightmare for introverts. When I am at the end of group B or group C, I know when I enter the plane there are a few certainties I will face:

1. Everyone—absolutely everyone will have their eyes on some portable electronic device, book, or magazine. People will even close their eyes so they won't have to make eye contact with you, and then you won't ask them if the seat next to them is taken.

2. There will *only* be middle seats available. Which means not only are you uncomfortable the entire trip to wherever you are going, you will start off the flight before you even reach your seat feeling uncomfortable because you are forced to walk the aisle looking for that weak passenger who will wilt at your stare and allow you to pass into the middle seat with nothing more than a glance.

3. You will be known by all who see you enter as the rookie traveler. Being at the back of the pack is a signal that you are the traveler who did not check in on time. You are the customer who has no idea what Southwest Airlines is all about. You are the passenger who is at the bottom of the food chain.

This, my friends, is what you get when you fly Southwest. And they aren't even cheap anymore. In the past, at least, you could console yourself in knowing there was a trade-off. Feel like a sardine? Well, at least you didn't get robbed for the privilege. Okay, rant over ...

On this particular occasion I was on Delta—the promised land of airlines. I was the fifth person on the plane, but somehow this dude was in the aisle seat *already*. Seriously. Laptop open, wires hanging all over the place. My immediate thought was: *Rookie.*

"Hey, man. Looks like you are the lucky guy. I'm sitting next to you."

This is the line. I use it weekly. If someone is in the aisle seat, this is my standard greeting. Nine times out of ten the person smiles and makes a lame joke back at me, then gets up, lets me in, and we are on our way to BFF status. This guy didn't even look at me. He just sort of made this half-grunt, half-puffing sound and packed his PC up only to stand, not even moving into the aisle, which meant I had to awkwardly slide in sharing a moment that was *way* more intimate than I cared to have with this PC-packing fifty-year-old. Good thing I only had four hours next to him.

If you are not a frequent flyer, these sorts of things are not a bother to you. They are an infrequent inconvenience that is not significant enough to merit a comment. But to me, my friends, this was the straw that was gonna break something. I don't own a camel, so I'll just say it broke my spirit.

I had just finished a weekend of performances—singing in twelve services over two days. I was spiritually, emotionally, and physically done. Exhausted. There was nothing that could have made this day any longer. Oh, except for this guy. I tried to make small talk. I got one-word answers. Okay, dude. Whatever. I'm out.

With that, I used my God-given gift and proceeded to sleep for the next three hours and forty-five minutes of the flight. That is, until around the three hour and forty-six minute mark of the flight when I woke up about three inches above my seat. Something along the lines of *Lost* was going down.

I'd watched TV enough to know that they always make everything look so much more dramatic on television. They can make overhead bins explode open almost simultaneously, spilling their entirety all over the passengers below. I've flown enough to know that people don't *actually* fly from their seats and hit their heads on the ceiling panels. Why, then, may I ask was I awakened by this kind of chaos? Why was all of this happening right now? I was pretty sure I wasn't still asleep. I mean I could feel my stomach in my throat.

"Ladies and gentlemen, this is the captain speaking. The winds from Hurricane Sandy are definitely whipping across, above, and below us. Even on the ground in Atlanta we have 40 mph gusts on the runway heading east to west, which means we will be landing in some heavy crosswinds. This is right on the verge of the winds being too high for us to land so we may have to divert to Chattanooga."

I knew one thing immediately: I was a fan of the Chattanooga idea. The fact that the pilot was *so* specific about this made me wonder how confident he was about landing in Atlanta. Then he piped in one more time:

"Or I may just try it ..."

Hold tight ... Try it? ... *Try it?* Listen, Captain. There is no try-ing anything here. I've fought far too many battles in life for you to take a gamble on anything other than a sure thing right about now. No trying. Just landing.

What was funny is that I never panic on planes. I have been through turbulence that makes the Scream Machine at Six Flags seem like a first-grade pony ride. Even this turbulence, although fierce, wasn't gonna faze me.

But then ... I looked left.

Bro was *not* okay. Remember him? The guy from a few para-graphs ago who was not into me at all? He was *so* not into me. And right about now he needed me more than he knew—hands gripping the seat in front of him and head resting on his right forearm and turned toward me. I tried desperately to get a stealth pic of him, but his eyes were staring straight out my win-dow. Eyes that were terrified. My mind fought against what I knew needed to be said. My mind fought against the moment that had to be had.

Moment Makers (that's you), there are times when you sneak into a moment without knowing it's even there. Those are the mo-ments you see on that TV show *What Would You Do?* with John Quiñones. You're sitting at a table at a restaurant and you hear a mom verbally abusing her fifteen-year-old teenage daughter. Or you're walking down the road and you see a young woman crying.

Yeah, those moments are the ones where it's easy to know what to do. But let me restructure them ...

You're sitting at a table in a restaurant and you hear a teen-age daughter verbally abusing her thirty-five-year-old mother. Or you're walking down the road and you see a drunk, homeless man crying. *Or, you are sitting on a plane and a fifty-year-old PC-packing grumpy man is having a panic attack next to you. Ugh …*

Suddenly I realized why he was such a pain earlier. He was petrified. He was petrified even before this 24 million-ton chunk of metal went hurling into the sky. He didn't talk to me because he was probably doing his breathing exercises.

And with the pilot's assurance of an "attempted landing" … well, it sent dude into a panic.

"Hey, man," I said, "it'll be okay."

Five words. Five words I didn't want to say but said anyway … and so fell the dominoes.

"Seriously, man. Just breathe."

At this point we were about thirty seconds from touchdown, and I did something I never would have imagined doing. I simply laid my hand on my left leg, palm up, and opened it. That's it. Didn't say a word.

I didn't even think he saw it. That is, until I felt a palm that was about 200 degrees Fahrenheit and soaking wet connect with it. He sat up, didn't squeeze, just rested it there, and closed his eyes. This moment lasted about twenty seconds. Twenty seconds filled with these thoughts:

Did he really just grab my hand?

He did. He really did just grab my hand.

Okay. He grabbed my hand. Now what?

Do I move my hand?

Do I do that rub my thumb against the top of his hand thing like I do with my kids to let them know it's gonna be okay?

When do I let go?

Do I look at him?

Do I say anything?

He's STILL HOLDING MY HAND.

You know what you do, Carlos?

You rest your hand on your leg and let him rest his hand in your hand until he lets go.

That's what you do.

And that's what I did. I sat there letting him hold on until we were safely on the ground. It was the sort of landing where everyone cheers when we touch down. And the passengers did not disappoint. At one point, about ten feet from touchdown you could literally see the entire plane shift about twenty feet to the left. And that was the moment it went from a landing that deserved a golf clap to a landing deserving of a " 'One Shining Moment,' last-second, NCAA, desperation-three-pointer-to-win-the-game, sixteenth seed upsets the #1 seed" kind of clap.

If there'd been nets on the runway, we would have cut them down.

I cheered. He said nothing—nothing at all. I wanted to say something, but there was really nothing to say. He didn't even look at me. He simply packed his bags and waited until it was our turn, stood up, and walked down the aisle.

So after getting off the plane, I followed the guy out onto the concourse. He wasn't about to turn around, which was fine by me. But then he looked over his shoulder—no expression—and simply locked eyes with me for a second. I don't know what he was thinking in that moment, but I know what I was thinking . . .

You needed to hold my hand 'cause you were scared. I needed to hold your hand 'cause it was selfish not to.

I realized that I needed to open myself to sharing the moment with him, making myself vulnerable, making myself receptive to what I could learn from the experience. As it turned out, opening my hand equaled opening my heart.

I don't even remember him letting go of my hand. All I remember is being in the air, holding the hand of a complete stranger, and then cheering and high-fiving the intoxicated lady behind me. And that wasn't really a "thing" until later that night in bed, when I was staring at the ceiling trying to remember what had happened on that plane. Then the significance of that moment hit.

That, my friends, was a Received Moment. Yes, I did something for my buddy by extending a hand in support, but by doing what I didn't really want to do for someone else, I received my own moment of meaning and significance.

As you set out on this journey of Moment Making you will discover that things rarely go according to plan, and that's not necessarily a bad thing. The most important thing is that the unexpected is actually a gift. It presents opportunities to take that moment you meant to make for someone else and allow God to put his spin on it. Allow God to breathe on it. When you open yourselves to the new, you open yourselves to unforeseen possibilities. It's there, right there, that we find our ability to grow and explore!

Remember when you were first learning to ride a bike? For some of you this may not have been the case, but for many of you I bet it was. When my dad taught me to ride a bike we were in a parking lot at Stone Mountain near Atlanta.

There were no cars, only wide-open space. I remember my dad walking alongside me, holding the back of the bike as we slowly moved from parking space to parking space. I remember feeling him supporting the bike—feeling him keeping me from falling. I could literally feel when he loosened his grip on the bike.

"Dad! Don't let go!" I would yell in a panic.

And he didn't—at least not until we got some speed under those tires. I remember the next moment as clear as day. I remember saying something to my dad as I was barreling down the parking lot and getting no response from him.

I remember saying it again … nothing. And then I remember rounding the corner and seeing my dad about sixty yards away with a smile brighter than the noonday sky. Wait! Why is he *there* and not *here*? *I was riding a bike!*

All it took was his hand holding my bike until he knew I didn't need it anymore. It was a moment he created for me, yes, and it was necessary for me to find safety and then find freedom.

What I needed was the hand on the back of my bicycle seat. What my friend on the plane needed was a hand under his hand. What we both needed was for judgment to cease so we could remember that we were all in the same predicament. We were all on the same plane going down.

That initial act is all that is needed sometimes to induce the little bit of bravery in someone that will set them free. These moments are received when we *explore* possibilities outside our comfort zones. And when we receive them with an open heart and an open mind they become the path between Created and Received Moments—the moments where we go from trying to do something for someone else to finding the message that was really in there for us. Sometimes all it takes is an open hand.

CHAPTER 6

RECEIVING FOCUS

You may be detecting a pattern by now ... I like sitting by windows. I especially like the table next to the bank of windows along the eastern wall of my neighborhood Starbucks—the big table—the one with the little blue disabled sticker at the far right corner. (I've never seen a brother in a wheelchair in there, but the second I do, I'll give him my seat.) I like it 'cause it's the most brilliant seat in the cafe.

From there you are positioned close enough to the door to catch a glimpse of everyone entering and far enough from the noise of the espresso machine.

When a storm rolls in you feel as though it is going to swallow you whole since the windows are thin enough to feel the vibration as the water hits the glass. Sometimes I go in just to watch a storm roll by. The rain always seems to be coming straight at me.

What is it about windows and rain that creates magic? I remember going through the car wash as a five-year-old kid. I was terrified of the noise. Every time Pops would turn left off Briarcliff Road to get gas instead of right, I knew I was in trouble—left was the Shell station, and the only reason we went to the Shell station was because we were gonna go into the mouth of the monster: the

Car Wash. *Humongous teeth swishing back and forth waiting to devour you.* They pounded on the windows and the roof of the car.

My dad would always tell me: "Carlitos, it's okay. You'll be okay. Just watch the water slide down the window." I never understood why he thought this would help when just avoiding the car wash was a much more effective solution. But it worked. I focused so much on the bubbles and the water sliding down the windows that, for a moment, I forgot about the dragon's teeth trying to rip through the roof of our car. I learned that the protection of those windows was far greater than I thought. And suddenly I was not scared anymore.

And the window in this Starbucks, during a good storm, gives me exactly that same feeling. Limbs and branches may flop against the windows, but the beauty of the water falling is gorgeous.

I also like watching the baristas do their thing. "Hey! Welcome to Starbucks!" Every single time. Like clockwork. And it's not only the ambiance. It's also Adam. Adam is a barista in his early thirties with a beard that would make Kimbo cry mercy. (Who's Kimbo? *Kimbo Slice.* The most ferocious YouTube street fighter known to man.) This beard was almost an entity in and of itself. This thing was, oh — maybe a foot long. Manly. And smelly, I'm sure. Adam's face is dominated by that beard. It's him. He is it. I only know Adam's features from the nose up. The rest of his face is beard.

So, needless to say, when I walked in one time to grab my Venti Skinny Hazelnut Latte (I know, not really a manly drink), I did a triple take when I saw Adam. Without his beard. *Without his beard!* I didn't know what to do. I smiled, gave some really horrible word of affirmation, and walked quickly to my seat.

Adam chuckled his 6'3" chuckle and said, "Different, huh?"

I was like, "Whoa. Dude. Why? I mean, cool. But, wow."

By this point Adam knew I was officially out of words, and if

I used "dude" one more time I would have morphed into Keanu Reeves.

"I had that beard for twelve years. Not many people have seen me without it. My wife's never seen me without it. My two kids have never seen me without it. I just thought it was time for a change."

"You ain't lyin', dude, it is a change," I said, once again resorting to my Southern California safety net of a fourth-grade noun.

I currently have an Abe Lincoln chinstrap beard. I've had that bad boy going on fifteen years. But it's cut short to my face, and when I do shave it off, which I do on occasion, people only look at me quizzically and say things like, "Did you shave your head? Did you lose weight? There's something different, I just don't know what it is." Even my kids. It will take them a moment, but then they realize that I buzzed it off and immediately run to start kissing my face all over.

Okay, okay. So maybe I shave it off only to have their cute little lips slobber all over my face. But my kids aren't scarred by my choice to shave. I'm thinking that since Adam's face was about 20 percent skin and 80 percent beard, his kids flipped.

"What about your kids? Did they freak?"

Adam responded with this story: "You know, Carlos, I thought really long and hard about that. I mean they are six and four. They have only known their father with a beard, yet that is only one way of looking at me. I am still me without my beard. They have just never experienced me this way. So you know what I did? I guided them through shaving my beard for me. Yes, with their tiny six- and four-year-old hands in mine, we removed the hair on my face. They never looked away, always gazing into my eyes. That way they could see that my eyes were still my eyes and I am still their dad. Nothing was changing. About halfway through, my oldest got a bit bored and wanted to go finish his movie. I didn't let him. They were not done with the change yet. I told him he had to finish. Once we were finished, well, they never flinched. It was as if they had always seen me this way."

When he finished his explanation I think my mouth was gaping about a quarter of the way open, and I was entranced by the poetry that just escaped from my friend Adam's heart. Was he a pastor in disguise? Did he honestly just drop that sermon on me without knowing? Did he just deliver to me one of the most groundbreaking moments of my life? A moment that literally shifted how I would handle change and transition from that moment forward? Certainly this man was some sort of prophet.

I quickly snapped out of my haze and offered something about how much younger he looks and how I wish I could grow a beard like his, but the bald spot on my middle left cheek would do me in. I was mumbling words, but all I could think about was the amazing word picture he just painted for me of my relationship with my Savior King.

All of a sudden, it started to come together for me. I started to understand how when I look away from God in times of chaos, and then look back up and the sun is hitting him from a different direction, I freak and think he's changed. I doubt. I run. I fear. I'm confused. All the while he's telling me, *Carlos, it's me. Don't look away, son. Stare at me through this mess in your life, and you'll see that I am the same yesterday, today, and forever. I may look different because of the way people paint me through their sermon series, worship songs, Bible translations, and consumer Christianity. But I promise you, son, stare into my eyes and know I hold you and will never leave you and never change.*

Think about how this plays out between Jesus and his disciples. Luke 8 brings us to the point of choosing to stare into trust or stare into fear.

Jesus and his disciples had been traveling from town to town doing ministry — miracle after miracle, healing after healing. I wonder at what point seeing miracles from Christ himself became a thing of normalcy for the disciples? Why would I assume that they became callous to it? Because of what went down in verses 22 to 25.

Jesus says, "Let's go to the other side of the lake, guys," and off they went. This next little detail about Jesus did not go unnoticed in my book. He fell asleep. Listen, stick me in a plane, train, or automobile and I'm out like a light. A boat only takes it to a whole other level. I can definitely sleep on a boat, but I don't think I would sleep through a *squall* coming down on the lake.

This wasn't the Titanic, people. This was a boat made of wood by the hands of fisherman. Anything with the name *squall* would most certainly take it out. And as this storm hit, the disciples did what any sensible men would do—they panicked. I can imagine it now:

"*Holy cow!* Where in the world is *Jesus*? How is he sleeping! Wake him up! That way we can die together and not alone!"

Panic. Jesus wakes up and rebukes the wind and the waters. If the winds and waters had feelings I'm sure they would be sucking their thumbs. Whenever I get rebuked I immediately shy into cowardice. And apparently the storm and the winds were no different. Then he asks the guys, "Where is your faith?" And I'm sure they replied with, "Okay. Okay. Never again. That's the last time we are gonna doubt you, Lord. The *last time!*"

And then, in Matthew 14, there is Peter who tried to walk on water. It's like he graduated from fear of death into an overeager faith that he could do the impossible! But it took focus. Staring into the eyes of the Savior. You see, at first they were all terrified that Jesus was a ghost when they saw him coming to them across the lake. Walking on water wasn't something that they had seen done before. Not like the cable specials with David Blaine or Criss Angel. No. Those are illusionists. This is the Messiah. No tricks here.

"Take courage! It is I! Don't be afraid!" Then Peter, who reminds me a whole lot of my middle child, takes Jesus up on his bet. But not before throwing some lip in for good measure, "Lord, if it's you, tell me to come to you on the water!"

One word from Jesus: "Come."

And off the boat Peter went ... and he walked on water. Keeping focused on the eyes of Jesus Peter *walked on water*! But Peter let his humanity take over and began to think this probably wasn't a good idea and that he is about to die. Sinking. Sinking. Sinking. Then Jesus reaches out, delivers one of his hundreds of "O ye of little faith" lines that the disciples regularly got, and pulls Peter up.

Now at this point in the story Scripture skips back to Peter and Jesus climbing back in the boat, but I have a strong suspicion that Jesus and Peter spent a long moment in the water. Jesus whispering to Peter, "Just look into my eyes. I'm right here. I'm right here." Of course Scripture doesn't say that ... but we know a moment was made. And a moment was had.

When his followers took their eyes off of him, they lost their way. When they forgot what he looked like—what his true nature was—they thought he bailed on them in their hour of need, but they were the ones who left him. They were the ones who changed, who allowed their faith to change. But Jesus was there all along shouting, "Keep your eyes on me, Peter. *Keep your eyes on me, Peter!* The storm is raging but I, *I am here.*" I know that's not Scripture, but I'd like to believe that was what Jesus was yelling to Peter through the rain, through the storm.

All that went rushing through my head in a matter of seconds.

"Carlos? Los?" Adam brought me back into Ventiland.

"Oh. Yeah. Man. Dude. Wow. Yeah. That's rad. I like it, Adam. And I'm glad you had your kids see that through with you. You're a smart man."

Just then, what must have been thirteen junior high cheerleaders came in and all ordered while talking on their cell phones. Adam just smiled and served them graciously.

I go to that Starbucks because of the atmosphere. I get these really cool little moments when I experience the power of nature in a fishbowl setting. I am a spectator and it is awesome. I learned to enjoy the fishbowl way back in the car wash as the shower swirled around us. My dad taught me how to focus on the unchanging beauty held in the water streaming down our windows.

Much later I began to understand that no matter what storms rage around us, when we focus our eyes on God's unchanging love and protection, we can find peace and beauty in any setting. And when we do that—when we shut out the distractions and really listen for how God might be trying to talk to us through them— then we begin digesting what we need to take away from what seems to be a chance encounter. When we eat, we get the beauty of the flavor, but we don't get the nutrients of that food until we digest it, until we let the food do the work. It is in these moments that we truly gain *understanding* of what it all means.

Adam shaved his beard. He revealed his face. Not a world-changing event. But God revealed himself to me through that exchange, which did change *my* world.

I got up and left as soon as I could before this guy could represent Jesus to me three times in one night. Two was all I could take. First the beard, then not going insane from those high school girls on their cell phones.

On the way home I glanced in my rearview mirror. My beard is so poser, especially compared to Adam's. And don't think I'm not going to have my kids shave that bad boy off before the end of the week. It won't have the same effect as Adam's beard did. But I hope I can help them understand the gift of the moment I received from Adam.

To stare into God's face as we experience the circumstances of life and to be reminded that some things never change.

CHAPTER 7

RECEIVING INSIGHT

I have fascinating friends — friends who help write international peace treaties, friends who write bestselling books, friends who own world-renowned restaurants, friends who have won gold medals, friends who have governed states. And sometimes I sit in my 1,200-square-foot, three-bedroom condo with my family of five in Nashville, wondering if my life is all that fascinating. I get sucked into the lie that the grass is always greener. There is always more somewhere else. That for some reason, fascinating equals accomplishments. I honestly wrestle with that ... that is, up until about a month ago when I met a seal. Let me explain.

My friend Bob lives in this magical place. It is a place that is not only magical because of the beauty that it spills on you every waking moment, but because everyone who goes there seems to come back transformed. It is located in this beautiful inlet nestled among peaks in beautiful British Columbia. Every so often Bob will invite a few friends to come and rest at this magic spot. And this summer I was lucky enough to be able to go and do just that.

There is no mobile phone coverage there. There is no internet service there. The only thing you'll find is good food, good conversation, and the Good Lord. On the second morning we were all sitting along this cliff overlooking the inlet, and my friend Don was talking to us about how we are all masterpieces. We are all true masterpieces, and all of this beauty around us—the peaks, the trees, the cliffs, the water—was all created for our enjoyment. That somehow we are the pinnacle of God's creative genius, and we're more fascinating than even this view could measure up to. I literally mumbled under my breath, "Yeah, right."

I mean how in the world could we be more beautiful and captivating than this place? The most beautiful place my eyes had ever seen. Don continued into other thoughts, and I'm sure there were fantastic points about how we are made in God's image, but all I could think about was how unfascinating I felt. I was obsessed with the idea that it *had* to be a lie that I am somehow more of a masterpiece than these mountains. I simply could not handle that truth at that moment.

About fifteen minutes after our group huddle on the cliff I was dropped off on this small stretch of rocky beach, no more than twenty yards wide and about ten yards deep. Boulders and rocks covered the beach, and I was once again surrounded by the most amazing beauty I had ever seen.

I was alone. As alone as I had probably been in . . . well . . . ever. Behind me was sheer cliff, and in front and around me was cold glacier water. "Find God, Carlos!" Bob yelled as he drove the boat away.

I took my shirt off, found a large flat rock, and lay down. *God, why do I fight this fight? Why can't I just be okay with me? Why must I always try to be more?*

The thoughts were racing through my head, so I grabbed my journal and started writing. It was a furious pace, and I must have covered close to four pages in four minutes. The entire time I was bawling my eyes out. The pages were stained with tears that seemed to have been meant for this situation alone—not wanting to feel the pain of not being enough.

I wrote fast and hard until my eyes could not make out the words my hands were creating anymore. I stopped and screamed, "JUST MAKE ME BELIEVE I'M A MASTERPIECE!"

And just like that, the intensity of emotion subsided as quickly as it had risen. I just sat there, head bent, still not feeling like a fascinating masterpiece but grateful I got to get all that out.

I stood up, dizzy from my emotional dramafest and decided to climb the rock about ten yards away from me. It was a boulder about five feet tall, and I felt like maybe I could see a little farther standing on top of that thing.

I struggled to the top and looked out. And ... I pretty much could see the exact same thing. It was only five feet after all. I'm such a seven-year-old sometimes with my lack of perception. But what escaped my lungs next was like the scream of a seven-year-old girl.

As I was beginning to climb down the boulder back onto my little stretch of secluded beach, I happened to catch movement below me. I focused my attention toward my feet and saw what had to be a seven-foot-long seal. *Only feet in front of me!*

These things look so cute at SeaWorld. They look so squishy and soft and cuddly on the other side of the glass where their trainers toss them little fishies so they behave. In the wild they aren't so harmless looking. I froze.

My head began swimming with thoughts like: *This seal is large. Larger than I am. I am obviously standing on its beach. I have the face of a mountain directly behind me. Can't climb it. I have water surrounding the other three sides of me. There is no doubt he is a faster swimmer. Should I just lay flat on the ground and allow him to finish me off now or do I put up a fight?*

I'm dramatic. I know. But I was mortified. I slowly backed up, hoping he/she/it didn't notice me. The only thing I figured I had going for me was all the wailing I was doing which probably made it deaf.

All it took was one step and pop. Its head popped right up, and it stared at me. I saw what he was thinking: *Big fish. Lunch!* And before I could jump off the boulder, the stare-down was over faster than a knife fight in a phone booth. (I've been waiting to use that line this entire book. Thank God I found the moment.)

I stumbled off the boulder and grabbed a handful of rocks, 'cause, you know, I was gonna scare it with a rock and stuff. I turned back to the water, surveying every square inch of the inlet hoping to see my "friend" a hundred yards away heading to eat someone/something else. Instead, I see Mr. Seal pop his head up close to shore. He stared at me. Right at me. We locked eyes, and he literally cocked his head left with an almost quizzical look.

I was taken aback. Fear turned into wonder. Wonder turned into amazement. And for the next twenty to thirty minutes this seal did not leave my line of sight. He swam back and forth. Back and forth. He never took his eyes off of me.

About ten minutes into this dance, God Almighty, the creator of the universe himself, screamed as loudly and as clearly as I've ever heard him speak. "*You are a masterpiece, Carlos. You are fascinating, Carlos.* This seal cannot take his eyes off of you. He does not know your insecurities. He does not know your social-media accomplishments. He does not know your professional accolades. He knows nothing about you. But he is completely and totally fascinated with you." And I began to weep.

With every blink of Mr. Seal's long lashes I settled farther and farther into the realization that I was being marveled at by a marvelous creature in the midst of God's marvelous landscape.

Game. Set. Match. Stick a fork in my unfascinating insecurities. They are done.

It took the sound of an approaching motor to scare my friend away. I saw the boat coming from at least half a mile away, and Mr. Seal saw it too. Off he went. Still popping his head up every twenty yards or so as he swam away from the shore, just making sure that the most fascinating human on planet earth was still there—or wishing this chunk of mass would leave his bedroom. Nonetheless he kept checking. I grabbed my camera and took as many pictures of my new friend as I could. Nobody was going to believe what happened to me. Nobody. I had danced a mental waltz with a seal. I had done what I thought was the impossible.

* * *

I know twelve or so guys who probably had this feeling before. They were a bunch of ordinary, unfascinating individuals who in a moment, were thrown into a life of Moment Making reserved for only the greatest of adventurers. These were some ordinary dudes. Matthew 10 calls them by name:

> Simon (who is called Peter) and his brother Andrew; James son of Zebedee, and his brother John; Philip and Bartholomew; Thomas and Matthew the tax collector; James son of Alphaeus, and Thaddaeus; Simon the Zealot and Judas Iscariot, who betrayed him. (v. 2–4)

None of these men were scholars. None of these men were rabbis. None of them were anything above average. Yet these were the men he chose to walk alongside him and eventually walk on water, heal the sick, raise people from the dead, and commune with God Almighty himself.

How many times have we automatically disqualified ourselves from a life of Moment Making because we feel unimpressive? How many times have we disqualified ourselves from a lifestyle of Moment Making because we feel less than adequate?

In our society we tend to reserve the special title of Moment Maker for the scholars, preachers, and rock stars. When in reality, that is not who Jesus selected. So why is it that we select them above ourselves?

I received the gift of a moment on that beach by a seal. *A seal.* Not a rich seal. Not a famous seal. Just a seal. And this seal changed my life. How many times do we sit along the sidelines and wait for the rich, famous person to do the life saving and Moment Making? It's not supposed to be that way.

I don't care if you are a nurse, teacher, janitor, fast food worker, or CEO of a multimillion dollar company. God has created us *all* to be Moment Makers. Just as the twelve disciples were led on this extraordinary journey of making life-giving moments for people around them, we are also to make these moments. And we are also to receive them when we are given them. Even if it's by a seal.

As I climbed on the boat, my buddy Brian asked me, "How was it?"

"Oh, man. You'll never believe what happened to me. Life changing! I was sitting on this rock and ..."

Brian interrupted me.

"Did it have to do with a seal? 'Cause when I was swimming by my rock a seal came up to me ..."

At this point I was waiting for Tattoo to come off the mountaintop of Fantasy Island screaming, "The plane, the plane," because obviously Bob had to have hit some seal-releasing button at just the right time. I went *exploring* and found a moment beyond anything I could have imagined was possible.

I met a seal, and as Bob instructed when he dropped me off, I went and found God. And God gave me a moment where I knew nothing would ever be the same again. Receive the gift of moments with open arms. They just might change everything from this point on.

CHAPTER 8

RECEIVING FAITH

It was the first night of the Jeremy Camp tour. Lipscomb Arena—Nashville. My friends were there. My wife was there. My kids were there. It was the biggest night of this Christian artist's career. Only months earlier I was writing these songs in a basement, and now I was going to sing them on this stage and live on this bus and have people sing with me. Finally, here was the night when all my friends would see how the work was paying off.

The chorus to my song "We Will Dance" says,

We will dance, we will shout, we will let it out.
We will rise as the church, we will shout aloud.
There's no one like our God!

The instrumental break after the bridge and before the last chorus is a good thirty seconds. I like to get the crowd to put their arms around each other and start bouncing. Bouncing slowly but surely and on the beat. It looks phenomenal—like a giant amoeba about to pounce on its prey. Wait. Do amoebas have prey? Maybe a jellyfish waiting to strike. Yeah, that's it. It's a blast, and then the crowd *explodes* into dance when we hit the chorus.

I remember seeing my kids spinning and dancing their hearts out during "We Will Dance" with no shame in their game on the front row. It made this callous worship leader fill with joy. It was an amazing night. Little did I know it was about to get so much more amazing . . .

After getting off stage I immediately went into the corridor behind the stage looking for my family so they could tell me how awesome I was.

I saw them in the distance, and the closer I got the more certain I was that this was not the greeting I was looking forward to . . .

Sohaila, the eight-year-old, was crying and from a distance appeared to be getting a sharp tongue-lashing from Heather. Seriously? The first night of my big tour, and I'm going to have to spank somebody?

I walked up giving Heather the "can you tell me what is happening without actually speaking?" look. This is something that newlyweds don't yet understand. Telepathy actually begins to occur after the first child. Thank God for this gift. She looked at me and then said, "Sohaila, go ahead. Tell Daddy why you're crying."

I immediately put on my "If I Have to Spank You Just Know I Love You" face. And poor Sohaila tried to tell me, but she was in the middle of that post-hard-cry breathing spasm. You know the one where you talk but are gasping for air every five seconds. She was at that place and not in a condition to tell me what had just happened . . .

I tried to help her out, "Sohaila, baby. Just breathe. Okay? It's gonna be okay. Whatever you did, remember, Daddy still loves you. Daddy loves you no matter what. Even through your bad decisions. Even when you do something like you just did. Daddy may be mad or a little disappointed. But this does not mean I don't love you. Okay? Okay?" How's that for parenting skill. Move over Super Nanny.

Then she laid it on me, "Daddy. When you were singing that last song, I felt so happy. But it was weird. I was happy because I felt Jesus, but it made me cry. Have you ever cried because you were happy? And I'm still crying because I felt Jesus telling me that I need to become a Christian." Insert screeching tires sound.

Remember that parenting high-five I just gave myself? Yeah, I had to take that back. "Um. Oh. Wow. Okay. Wow. Really? So. What do you need, baby? How can Daddy help you with these feelings?" I stumbled through my words with little more skill than a nervous pageant girl.

"Daddy. I want to become a Christian. Can you pray with me?"

Sooooo, the whole speech about whatever you just did that will make Daddy mad and disappointed ... that speech? Is there a rewind button anywhere? I immediately started wondering where the closest children's pastor was. Where was her church small-group leader when I needed her? I needed a tract. Where were those ABCs to becoming a Christian? Can someone *please* show up so I don't screw this up?

Then my mind went here:

What did I say on stage to confuse her? Did I trick her?

I know I probably said something that manipulated her into thinking it was Jesus when it was really me and my bad theology. I am sure that I sang the last stanza of "Just As I Am" too long. Wait. I didn't even sing that song. I know I did something. Help me, Jesus.

So I started at her:

"Okay, Sohaila. So, you understand, this isn't a feeling, this is a relationship; this isn't a one-time thing, it's a life of devotion. This isn't something to do just because you think Daddy or Mommy wants you to do it. This isn't something that you do just to go to heaven. Because you know you are going to live here on earth a lot longer, and, well, don't become a Christian just for heaven. You know it's about more than heaven, right? You know that heaven isn't really filled with gold and stuff. I mean, sure. There will be gold there. And you know that heaven isn't really in the clouds. Like it's not some city just floating in the clouds, right?"

And about three minutes into my salvation spiel verging on *Twilight Zone* meets *The Fringe* she stopped me.

"Daddy. I just love Jesus. And I want him all the time. I just love him so much and want everyone to feel the way he makes me feel."

Out of the mouth of babes ...

So she prayed. Not repeating a prayer after me, just her thoughts to God.

"Dear God, I just love you. I've been wanting to tell my daddy this since I was six. I love you so much. I love you so much. Amen."

Like a scene from some epic children's movie, the second she started praying, John Mark, on stage, started singing "How He Loves." When Sohaila said, "Amen," she looked at me and started singing with him. She knows every word. At that moment there was not a whole lot separating "Jesus Loves Me" from John Mark's "How He Loves." Such a simple truth. Such perfect timing.

We try and put so much in between our children and God to make sure they "get him" when the truth is they are often closer to him than we are on our closest days.

All she needed was to see her father worshiping God. All she needed was to see her father dancing unashamed in front of a bunch of Nashville spectators. And she joined with me. No tracts. No Disney production. No four weeks of meeting with a pastor. Just me, her, and Jesus.

* * *

I think of when Jesus was with a group of grown-ups and a crew of kids crashed the party. I'm sure their parents were beside themselves with joy that the kids had a chance to sit at the feet of Jesus. And right when the kids sat down, here come the grumpy old deacons (cough), I mean disciples, to break up the party. It says the disciples "rebuked" them. And this wasn't the first time the disciples rebuked the parents for bringing in kids. *They did it all the time!* And Jesus dropped the, what I like to call, "Heaven Is Theirs and Not Yours" bomb. He said this, "Let the little children come to me, and do not hinder them, for the kingdom of heaven belongs to such as these" (Matthew 19:14).

Let's sit on that for a moment. Jesus just told his disciples, the men who had dropped their nets and left their families behind to follow Christ, that they had better learn right quick from these kids so that they get a piece of heaven too.

And in Matthew 11:25 he makes it pretty clear what he thinks about who gets him the best: "At that time Jesus said, 'I praise you, Father, Lord of heaven and earth, because you have hidden these things from the wise and learned, and revealed them to little children.'"

I may not have banned the kids from the service, but I made almost as much of a mess of things. I was so concerned about making this moment with Sohaila just right—so concerned about making sure she did it right—that I almost blew it and robbed her of a simple moment with her Savior. Jesus knew that the uncomplicated faith of children leads to a much more honest experience than so much of the contrived worship we try to put on. His moment of pure connection with those little kids was more powerful and would have a longer-lasting impact than any grand miracle or deep sermon ever would.

I should have known better with Sohaila. I didn't need to find the right thing to say. I didn't need to set the stage. I didn't need to be concerned about authenticity, sincerity, or her level of comprehension. I didn't need to do anything more than be in the moment—with her.

After she prayed her prayer, and John Mark struck up the band exactly on cue and made me cry like a little girl, she said, "Dad,

I like the happy cry. It makes me feel good." I like the happy cry too, kid.

The importance of *pausing* long enough to allow a moment to unfold without forcing it—giving it breathing room to become what it will—made this a Received Moment like no other.

CHAPTER 9

RECEIVING LIFE

Yeah, I thought she was gone. Somewhere around the third spin she looked at me, and it was bad. She looked scared. She was looking to me for help, but I had to hang on. I just wanted to hit Rewind. Those were the thoughts flying through my head seconds after we were T-boned in that intersection in downtown Atlanta.

It started as a wonderful early weekend with my boy Eric and his wife, Angela, and their kid, Landon. I was back in Georgia for the first time since moving to LA with my wife, Heather. It was going to be a short trip but full of friends and laughter. A wedding weekend. One of my best friends, Inman, was getting married. He had landed a beautiful bride.

Friday was the rehearsal. The dinner was amazing, and Heather and I were having so much fun. She was being her witty self, and I was her comedic partner. We were on. It was awesome. This was the most fun we'd had so far in our two-month marriage. Yeah, two months. Still newlyweds.

Saturday morning was special. We had breakfast with my brother, Eddie, and then chilled at his pad. He pulled a classic Carlos and locked his keys in his apartment. Once we got the keys,

Heather and I had to race off to catch up with my old friend Scott. We were meeting him at noon but had to be dressed for pictures at 12:30 p.m. So my baby and I were driving east on Briarcliff Road at about 11:40 a.m.

The road didn't make much sense as I was approaching the split. It forked, but we couldn't really tell where. Heather asked me which way the road went. If it went straight, then the oncoming traffic would not have to yield. But if it went left, then they should yield.

It happened so fast, but I remember everything. The car ahead of me forked left. That looked right, so I followed. The intersection was about thirty feet from the crest of a hill. No traffic in sight. But they would have to stop anyway. Then my girl screamed. I looked out her window and saw a Honda Accord flying over the hill. No brakes. No time. I gunned it. Too late.

Dear God. We got slammed. Heather was almost in my lap, and we were spinning. *Please, don't let her die.* We spun around three times. During the last spin we locked eyes and she needed me. *She needed me, Lord, and I was helpless.*

We slid off the road and down a fifteen-foot embankment. We flipped and landed on her side of the car. It was so quiet. Oddly serene.

She looked so peaceful. She seemed a little dazed, and we just stared at each other. It was dreamlike. Then like a flash . . .

Chaos ensued. The shock wore off and everything sped up. It was loud. People were screaming. *Don't let her die.* My door had dislodged in the collision; but my girl makes me buckle up, so I stayed secure. I released myself from the seatbelt and pushed the door open to climb out of my side of the car. I was okay . . .

I sprinted around to the other side. Three or four guys helped me push the car back on all four wheels. She was trapped. She had lost consciousness.

She was drooling. *I can't live without her.* I screamed at her. Shook her. Nothing. Everyone around me was panicked.

Then my girl decided not to quit. She opened her eyes, and I kissed her cheek. I asked her if she felt me. She forced a smile. She was crying. I told her not to leave me. She said she wouldn't. But she was in pain. The other car had smashed her almost all the way onto my seat. Her side of the car was nonexistent. I was terrified I was going to lose her.

The ambulance and fire truck showed up in about two minutes, from what I was told. To me it seemed like forever. They took over the rescue, seeing that our rescue had gotten us nowhere but me on my knees kissing her cheek.

They couldn't open the car. They took out that big yellow jaw thing but decided to climb in through my side and take her out. She was scared. I was panicked. But Lord knows I had to be strong.

"Mr. Whittaker?" I heard a voice behind me. It was a cop. A big cop — what I would consider a mean-looking cop.

"Umm, yes, sir! Over here! That's me! This is my wife! Please tell me she's gonna be okay." I was obviously a hot mess.

"Sir, are you the owner of this vehicle?" the cop asked.

"Umm. Yes. I mean, no. We are from California. I'm just borrowing it for the weekend from a friend. Umm. Can I go back to my wife?" I replied.

"Not yet, son. I have a few more questions."

Yes. You are reading correctly. This man was questioning me while my wife lay dying in the passenger side of a car only a few feet away.

"You were the one driving the vehicle, correct, Mr. Whittaker?" he asked.

"*Listen, man!* My wife is hurt over there! Can you ask me these questions later?" And seconds later I found myself in handcuffs in the backseat of an Atlanta Police Department squad car. *This can't be real.*

Through the glass protecting the cop in the front seat from dangerous criminals like me, and through my tears, I could see them finally pull Heather from the wreckage. I could see them start working on her. That's when my brother showed up.

"You get my brother out of the inside of that cop car right now!" he lashed out at the cop.

"Young man, I'm going to give you one more try," he replied to my brother.

Thank God, Eduardo calmed down long enough to realize getting both of us arrested wouldn't help the situation. Through the chaos of the moment the cop actually thought I had stolen the car. About two minutes later, the cop let me out, and I literally fell limp into my brother's arms.

I was drained. I had nothing left. I needed my brother more than ever, and I was so grateful he was there. They were putting her in the ambulance when I got my first sign that my girl was going to be okay. She called my name. I ran to her. She asked me where her camera was. *You have got to be kidding me!*

I had just seen them *cut* her out of the car. She was on a stretcher, and the paramedics did not have a look of peace on their grills. No. They were visibly stressed. And she wants me to take a picture.

I said it didn't matter where the camera was. She told me exactly where to look for it: on the floorboard on her side of the car. "Go get it and take a picture for my scrapbook!"

Eddie and I just looked at each other. *Her scrapbook?* Seeing that there was a good possibility this could be a dying wish, I obliged. I ran over to the car. I started digging through the wreckage looking for this stupid camera—the camera that would take the last picture of my wife on this earth.

Reluctantly, I ran back to the ambulance and took her picture as she smiled, strapped to that board. Only Heather—our Moment-Making Director/Producer.

So the ambulance took off, and I was going to my brother's car when I saw our car one more time. From the wreckage I could tell she was not going to be the same physically. I knew that, but I was going to love her more. She might not even make it, but I would still love her more. I needed to go see my baby. Glass. Smoke. Cell phones. Tears. Blood. Gasoline. God. Peace. Horror. Peace. Love. Peace.

As I burst into the ER I learned they had already taken her to stop the bleeding in her brain and lungs. I had to wait. So I walked outside and started calling. Her parents. My parents. My church family back in LA. Everyone.

By the time I walked back into the hospital, Heather was back in the ER. I rushed to her and she smiled. The doctor pulled me to the side along with the three ambulance workers. He looked me square in the eyes and told me that he was pretty amazed. Heather had no broken bones. No internal bleeding. No brain bleed. Just a major concussion. We were lucky to be alive, he said.

I knew right then that our God is bigger than anything. He wrapped something around our car that morning. He wrapped something around Heather's body that morning. And He unwrapped the blindfold from around my eyes that morning. My eyes got a glimpse of God I hadn't let myself see before. Something big was revealed to me in that moment.

Later, when I walked into the hospital room, she looked at me and said, "Baby, I can't remember if we are married. Are we married?" She lost all memory of the week. She asked me whose wedding we were going to probably five thousand times. And each time, I answered her as though it was the first. She was also high as a kite on pain meds, but she was going to be okay. Throughout the night we had all sorts of visitors. Even the bride and groom showed up *straight from the wedding*—wedding dress and all. Old friends I hadn't seen in years were piling in to pray for us. And the whole time, she couldn't remember what had happened just five minutes before.

I got a dry-erase board and started writing everything down that had happened on that board so she could remember. It was like *50 First Dates*, but before the movie.

This was a moment that I obviously wish I could forget—the moment where I almost lost my best friend because of something I did. But I learned something critical in the moment I will never forget. Life is short. Life is precious. We were reveling in the newness of our life together and celebrating the new life our friends were starting, and all of that could have been wiped out in a moment.

* * *

Jesus met with his disciples not long before his death and began pouring out his heart, trying to get them to see the urgency of living attentively and deliberately. He says to his closest friends, "Love one another." He reminds them that there is nothing that means more than that.

He knew that his time with them was short, and he needed to make sure the message was coming through loud and clear. He also knew that each of us only has a limited number of days we get to be here and that we can't afford to waste any of them.

So, even though that moment is one I would never wish on anyone, and one I would never want to relive, I am beyond grateful for the *understanding* that came from the moment. I was given an opportunity to learn a really important truth: His grace is sufficient. It really is.

Remember, we are only a whisper away from eternity. Look around. Who haven't you told about God's undying love?

CHAPTER 10

RECEIVING TRUTH

The day I tweeted that I was taking my wife, my eleven-year-old daughter, and my nine-year-old daughter to work tornado relief in Moore, Oklahoma, somebody tweeted back: "Why would you subject your children to something that could ruin their innocence?"

You know what? That almost changed my mind. It wasn't my idea anyway; it was Heather's. The Producer/Director of Moments in the family wanted to make this a teaching moment.

You see, a few years back I was the one who got to go to Joplin after a twister had completely flattened that town. I'd never seen anything like it. It was like two thousand steamrollers lined up in a row and started driving for miles absolutely destroying every-thing in their path. There was nothing left. I even sacrificed my body to help.

Not two minutes into job site number one, I lost my balance, stum-bled left, and felt a nail go through the bottom of my shoe, through my sock, through the first layer of skin, and all the way through my foot and out the top. I am sure you immediately wonder. *Did he REALLY feel it do all of that?* I answer your question with a simple and solid, *"Yes, it hurt all the way through and all the way back out."*

I stumbled over to the van and pulled off my boot. I had a bright red sock instead of a nice white sock. And just like that, I blew my plan to go in and make a difference. Two antibiotics and one *really long* tetanus shot later, I was good as gold. But I milked it for sure. After three days of hobbling around, struggling through exhausting work, we finally piled back in the cars and headed home.

Walking in the front door and trying to unpack the emotional, physical, and spiritual journey I had just gone through was impossible. I got frustrated that Heather wasn't more into my stories, and she was frustrated that I left her home with the kids while I went on a trip she really wanted to be part of. We realized that as a married couple this was the sort of trip we need to take together.

So this time, when the Oklahoma need came up, Heather was the one who was free, and I was the one with a book deadline. (Yes, the one you are currently reading . . .)

When our church organized a team of over sixty people to drive twelve hours from Nashville to Oklahoma City to help rebuild, I told her she needed to go, and I could see it all over her face that I was right.

What I assumed in that moment was that she would go and I would be at home with the kids. I would lock myself in my closet and type while I had Mr. Netflix babysit for the three days. It sounded like the perfect plan to me. Netflix all day, Chuck E. Cheese all night. (Chuck E. Cheese now has free Wi-Fi for all you parents not wanting to watch your kids as they contaminate themselves with the germs of millions of other sweaty little kids. It's fantastic. But I digress . . .)

But you know what? That was not what our family Moment Producer had in mind. (I'm the guy who proposes the adventures. Heather . . . she is the one who really makes the moments happen.) "I wanna bring the kids," she said.

Hold up. Hit the brakes. Slow down. Not my little girls. They were too small and innocent for something like this. This was not like taking them to a museum where they can see pictures of damage done by a tornado. This was taking them into the belly of the beast. And I knew, beyond a shadow of a doubt, that this was a bad idea.

Sohaila, my eleven-year-old, cries at the slightest whisper of pain and loss.

And I'm not talking about some massive pain or loss. I'm talking about her soul-crushing devastation over stepping on a naked Barbie in the middle of the night.

I'm talking about tears at the end of every year because she is sad that she will never see that year again. She is *not* gonna be okay with seeing the pain and suffering of these poor Oklahomans—our fellow humans.

The nine-year-old on the other hand, she is her mother. She is as hard as a rock. Her emotion comes out in aggression and neck rolls. She is fierce, and I suggest you get on her good side fast. I knew I wouldn't have to worry about her. Her sister is the one who, when I ask her why she is crying, answers, "I don't know, Daddy. I'm just emotional." Well, at least she's not a liar.

"Listen," my wife said, "the church we're partnering with— they have this huge warehouse where they will need volunteers to help organize donations. The girls can work there, and we can get a babysitter for Losiah. They don't have to go anywhere near the tornado damage. It will be okay. Trust me." And with that, not only was my entire family going, so was I.

I knew I needed to go to experience this with them. Even if I didn't have the time, this would be a moment we wouldn't forget. It just meant my publisher would have to wait an extra week to get this book.

"Girls, are you excited about going to Oklahoma to help the tornado victims?" I asked them. Half expecting to hear their tween reactions filled with 10 percent excitement and 90 percent

"Can't-We-Just-Stay-With-Our-Friends?" I got nothing of the sort. I actually got this: "Daddy. I saw the news. I can't wait to go and help clean up."

They wanted to be in the trenches!

"Baby, how about you just stay in the warehouse and help them organize? That's a powerful job," I told one of the two.

"No, Daddy. I want to help clean," she answered.

And that launched a big struggle inside my heart. It wasn't so much about the physical danger — although, that nail that went through my foot? Yeah, I was not about that happening to my girls. It was more about the emotional danger. Could their little psyches handle it?

Which brings me back to the tweet and the replies from countless followers telling me why I shouldn't take my innocent little girls. They almost changed my mind. They almost convinced me that they could not handle the devastation. They almost convinced me that they would somehow lose the innocence they have in their eyes. They almost me convinced that my girls would somehow hate me later in life for showing them the pain and suffering of this world. Then we went.

The bandanas they were using for masks to keep all the debris from filling their tiny lungs almost swallowed their entire faces. With sweat dripping off my nine-year-old's brow, she asked me through her bandana, "Daddy, where's the best spot to look for pictures?" *She wants her pictures? She's definitely her mother's daughter.*

We were standing on the remains of what used to be East Laurel Street.

And by "used to be" I mean that there was nothing left standing. It was completely flattened. The owner of one house walked up to me the moment our team arrived and said, "Thank you so much. I'm just so tired, and we have so much left to find. Thank you so much." All she could say was thank you, and all she wanted were family videotapes and pictures. She said nothing much else could be saved, but nothing much else mattered.

Well, that day our team found over fifty photos and countless VHS tapes for her. One picture in particular was of her husband standing next to her as she was holding a newborn baby, who, I assumed, was the young man on the east side of the house frantically digging for something. The kid was only hours old in the picture but was well into his teens today. I walked over to him. "Hey, buddy. This you?"

My wife and girls were in the kitchen area looking for stuff when I walked over to Seanna. "Baby, I'm so proud of you. I'm so proud of everything you've accomplished while you've been here. You've worked so hard. I'm so proud of you, baby." She thanked me and then immediately told me to move out of the way because I was standing in the middle of the pile she was working on.

Oh, my mini-Heather.

I saw my children shovel. I saw them hug. I saw them sift. I saw them serve. I saw them stack. I saw them laugh.

And then the last night we were there ... I saw *her* cry. No. Not the cryer.

The other one. The strong one. The mini-Heather. I saw her cry.

We had gathered for a final night of debriefing. We had a short devotion, and a local worship leader came out to lead us in worship. It was while we were singing, "And if our God is for us, then who could ever stop us? And if our God is with us, then what could stand against?" Her tiny nine-year-old arms were raised to the sky, and her tiny cheeks were the freeway for her tears.

That tweet came racing back to my mind as I asked her what was wrong ... and in that moment fear sprinted into my heart. But five seconds later fear was replaced with a Received Moment I won't soon forget. The gift of revelation so pure and so simple that only the mouths of babes can produce. She said, "I'm just sad, Daddy. They lost everything. I'm just sad."

Oh, yeah. It's sad. And it's okay to be sad. It's okay for *her* to be sad.

Sadness. Our creator wants us to feel that in moments like this. Moments where we need to be able to relate and feel what someone else is feeling. And it's okay. It's okay that she was sad.

We weren't going to run out the door of the church, into the twelve-passenger minivan, and go pick up a prescription of Paxil. This sadness, I believe, was placed in her tiny heart by God himself so she could be his hands and feet.

* * *

Jesus told his disciples that there would be suffering, but that they could endure it because there was something good on the other side of it:

> Very truly I tell you, you will weep and mourn while the world rejoices. You will grieve, but your grief will turn to joy. A woman giving birth to a child has pain because her time has come; but when her baby is born she forgets the anguish because of her joy that a child is born into the world. So with you: Now is your time of grief, but I will see you again and you will rejoice, and no one will take away your joy. (John 16:20–22)

Jesus is pretty much telling them—and us—that all of the sadness, all of the grief, all of the pain is okay because there is something on the other side. There is joy to come. Maybe it won't happen right away. Maybe it doesn't happen in this lifetime, but if you have him, it will come.

It's okay that she learned at nine years old what most kids her age in America won't soon learn—how to be the hands of the Healer.

When we left, I was convinced she could handle the devastation. I saw her handle it with a shovel in one hand and a rake in the other. I was convinced she kept the innocence in her eyes. I felt her squeeze over next to me in the middle of the night while she whispered, "Hold me, Daddy." Knowing that she could handle seeing the devastation because she knew she was loved and cared for.

Most of the time Received Moments hit you like a two-by-four across the forehead.

You can almost hear yourself gasp when they land. Think back for a second to the last one you had—the last gift of an awakening you experienced. You gasped, didn't you?

It's because, although it may not be a two-by-four coming across our domes, it is a two-by-four coming across our hearts. And when hearts change, direction changes, and when direction changes, lives change. That's why these Received Moments are so important to understand and acknowledge. If we just let them go by without examining them, we will miss *sooo* much of what was wrapped up in those puppies.

We miss the depth beneath the initial *aha.* I mean, who stops digging when they first find gold? Nobody in their right mind. They keep digging because there is more where that came from. More directly under the initial gold they found.

And in that moment, my nine-year-old showed me the "gold" that she can handle a little sadness. And that gold was just the beginning because as I kept digging I found this:

"Seanna? How do you feel right now? Do you like the way you feel? What other things could we do to help you feel this again?"

I dug and I dug. Every time I swung the pick I uncovered more gold—more gold than the simple truth that she is compassionate. Yes, I found that. But I also found a few layers of earth beneath that showed me she has a heart of empathy that she desires to uncover more often. She wants to feel this way more. She feels connected to God when the melody of music hits her at the same time as the melody of service. So as I went *exploring,* I found some amazing things. But most amazing? I found that my young, strong daughter can literally change the world.

PART THREE

RESCUED MOMENTS

I remember it happening when I was six. I was riding my bike down the gravel path behind Rehoboth Elementary School in Decatur, Georgia. The rocks seemed so much bigger as I was screaming down the hill, my friend Greer right on my tail. My tan and gold banana-seat racer was fresh out of the box. I could still see my dad's smile displayed proudly underneath his Tom Selleck mustache as I opened the package. It was my dream—as close to ecstasy as a seven-year-old in 1979 could feel.

We weren't rolling in the Benjamins. My dad worked for the Southern Baptist Convention, and that meant we were living off the tithes of a few devoted Baptists. So the fact that my dad went to Kmart and bought me this ride was above and beyond. I knew we could not afford the bike since my dad had already told me numerous times: *"Carlitos. No tenemos el dinero para comprar la bicicleta. Comprende hijo?"* That's Spanish for "It ain't gonna happen, Holmes."

And you know what? I was okay with that because I knew how hard my dad worked, and I knew how hard he had worked just to get us into a neighborhood where I could race nice middle-class white boys named Greer down a gravel path behind Rehoboth Elementary School.

My dad and I spent hours putting that bike together. I remember finishing it just as an episode of *The Dukes of Hazzard* was starting in the background. Bo and Luke, you have a new partner. Call Daisy. I'm on my way.

"Here I come, Carlitos!" Greer screamed. No way. I was not letting him beat me. I had dreamt of this moment for weeks. Ever since Greer had gotten his cobalt blue 1976 HMX. We were all sitting on the curb in the cul-de-sac in front of my house when he rounded left off of Sprucewood Drive. Bobby saw it first: "No way! He got it," Bobby whispered. We all looked up and there it was in all its glory.

Greer had been telling us for months he was gonna get it. None of us believed him. Nobody had seen a bike that blue in our collective twenty-one years on the planet. It was a Japanese BMX knockoff. But none of us cared about that. All we knew was that it was fast—the fastest in our neighborhood, the fastest on Rehoboth Hill.

Remember, my dad was a minister. I was his kid. I had a set of dimples Gary Coleman would be jealous of. My mini 'fro was parted perfectly down the right side of my dome. I could woo any Sunday school teacher in the country with the speed at which I found any Scripture they would spit out on a Sunday morning. I rolled my *r*'s when I said my name. I was that kid. I was perfection in the eyes of old Baptist ladies, and I knew it. I could do no wrong. As far as I knew, I was the perfect representation of what two parents could achieve. Yes. I actually believed this—until something happened in that straightaway down Rehoboth Hill that changed everything.

Greer and I rounded the first corner and hit a stretch of gravel where none of the neighborhood kids were watching. Scott, Brian, and Lee were at the bottom of the hill. Scott and Brian holding a bunch of sheets of the morning paper we had very carefully glued together to make a finish-line tape. Lee was the judge in case there was a photo finish. Greer and I? We were all alone. Just two seven-year-olds flying down a hill at what had to be a good ten miles an hour. We were the wind. The wind was us. Then it happened.

I peeked over my left shoulder to see Greer in his tuck position. He was gaining on me. There was no doubt about it. I knew he was gonna pass me, and I knew I had to act fast because we were about to turn the next corner and be in plain view of the three at the bottom. I began to hit my left hand brake, slowly and gently until I could hear his tires kicking rocks directly behind me. I slowed down a bit more and then I swung my left arm so hard it knocked him clear off his ride. I don't know if I hit chin or chest. I don't know if he landed on the rocks or in the woods. I just knew it was over and nobody saw.

Before I even rounded the corner off the straightaway I remember feeling guilt shoot down my legs and then back up my spine, eventually finding a seat in the middle of my throat. I was seven, and already I was no longer what everyone believed. I had done a serious wrong.

Then, clear as Fresno sky, I remember leaving the guilt behind me as I rounded the corner to hear the screams of my three fans. I tore across the finish line and waited for Greer to limp across.

"Where's Greer?" Scott asked.

"I don't know. I thought I heard him fall on the straightaway," I replied.

We waited. We waited longer. Nothing. He never did cross the finish line. I later found out that Greer had picked up his bike and walked through the woods back to his house. Greer never spoke to me again. When I say never, I mean, we spent the next three years living down the street from each other and even when we found ourselves playing on the same playground, I'd try to say hi, and he would completely ignore me. When it was time for the neighborhood Easter Egg Hunt, he would steer clear of me. I eventually moved to another neighborhood, and we went to different high schools, so my conscience got a break. But it never completely emptied out of my soul no matter how hard I tried.

Skip forward a few decades, and I am struggling as much today as I was then with the need to elevate myself on the back of someone I'm stepping on. Although not as fierce of a struggle, I still feel the temptation. Having children somehow opens your eyes to the pains of the world a bit more. But nonetheless, the battle still rages. When we do this, we not only injure someone else, but we injure ourselves. And we lose not just once, but twice.

The race on my new bike against Greer was the first moment I remember making a conscious decision to sin. I'm sure I sinned before then. Just ask my mom. Yet that was the moment I first lost the battle inside my heart.

What's fascinating is that right now, as I type these words, sitting at the corner table at my local Starbucks, I'm nauseated again. I think I'm disappointed not in seven-year-old Carlos, but in fourteen-year-old Carlos, in twenty-four-year-old Carlos, in the guy who never gained control of that need for acceptance. Little did I know how the simplicity of that moment could lead to me feeling invincible in my sin.

As I was preparing to write this story, I knew something needed to happen. Something I did not, in any way, shape, or form want to be part of. You know what needed to happen. We all know what needed to happen.

What needed to happen is that even twenty-nine years after a moment, *rescue* needed to happen.

See, here is the beauty of what I know. I know that even when a moment scars someone, even when a moment devastates someone, it is *never* too late to rescue that moment. It is never too late to see the arms of Jesus around a moment and allow him to rescue it. And so, with that, I take you to a few Sunday afternoons ago.

I'd led worship all morning here in Nashville. I got home and the house was quiet. The girls were at a birthday party, and Losiah and Heather were at the flea market. Perfect time for a nap. Perfect time for a little Carlos rescuing. But as life would have it, a real rescue trumps napping every time. It's been thirty years, guys. *Thirty* years.

Ready … aim … Facebook. It took me all of three minutes and forty-five seconds to find him. So I clicked Add Friend. Greer's profile was private, so I couldn't see where he lived, what he did, or anything else, for that matter. Nothing more than his profile pic. But I knew the second I saw him that this was Greer.

It was almost overwhelming to see his eyes—knowing what I had done and that he may or may not even remember; but also knowing what I had to do, if not for him, for me. Rescue.

I was prepared for a rejection or at least a few weeks of waiting. But minutes later I checked back and we were now Friends. Then I saw something that wasn't on my screen before my Friend request. A red number 1 attached to my inbox. I knew before I clicked it that it was from him.

> Carlos! Hey, man. How are you? Thanks for the friend request. I've loved keeping up with your life online via your blog and YouTube. I saw you on TV for that video of your kid. That was so funny. Hope all is well … Greer.

Seriously? Really? Can a man not even take the first kindness punch without someone stealing his thunder? Alas, this was the moment I would be working with. I replied.

Hey man! Thanks so much. I haven't even taken time to look through all your pics and catch up stalker-style. Hope you are well. Let me get right to the point. I'm sorry. Sincerely. There is a touch of ridiculousness in what I am trying to do right now; but on the Rehoboth Hill, on that hill, I lost the battle inside my heart. And I'm sorry, man. Sincerely. As a grown man with a wife and three kids, I'm sorry. This is an apology from a few people. It's an apology from seven-year-old Carlos who committed the act of cowardice. It's an apology from fourteen-year-old Carlos who would walk by you in high school like you didn't exist. It's an apology from twenty-four-year-old Carlos who saw you at Applebee's and remembered what happened like it was the day before, but still said nothing. And it's an apology from thirty-eight-year-old Carlos who needs it more than you do.

I'm sorry, friend. Thanks for hearing me out.

From zero communication to a Friend add on Facebook, and two messages exchanged in five minutes.

You know what I would love to be able to share with you right now? I'd love to be able to tell you I got this reply from Greer: "Hey, Carlos. Thanks for the note. Don't worry about it. I forgave you a long time ago. Hope you are well!"

But you know what? That's not the reply I got. Instead, I got nothing. Nothing at all. Silence.

It's been a while now. I've written him a few more times making sure he got my message, I've seen his Facebook feed filling up on a daily basis, but I haven't seen a reply. My mind raced with reasons to explain the lack of response, and I obsessed over it more than a few times. Then I realized something quite simple. It is rule number one for rescuing moments.

1. *You can only control the rescue, you can't control the rescued.*

Read that sentence again.

In spite of your best effort to rescue a moment, the moment may have been in the chilling and icy waters of your sin too long. The attempt to rescue a moment may not work. And sometimes you have to wait and see. Sometimes after a rescue you don't necessarily know if the rescued will survive.

I remember when I was a kid there was this little girl who fell down a well. The entire nation was glued to the television wondering if she would survive. And after a few days, she made it out. She was banged up and bloody, but she was alive. But we didn't know the full extent of her injuries. We had to wait for those.

The same thing happens with Rescued Moments. Even with our most valiant efforts, sometimes these moments will not have the stamina or strength to endure the pain they have already been through. But this does not mean that these moments should not be rescued. Out of respect alone, attempt the rescue.

I don't know if Greer is going to write me back. I don't know if he even wants to talk about it. I do know this though: I am certain that I did what I needed to do. I know that I couldn't be okay without walking back up the gravel path of Rehoboth Hill that brisk October day in 1979 and trying to pick Greer up off the ground. I didn't do it then. But I can do my best to do it now. And so can you.

There will be moments in need of rescue. Some of those moments are from this morning. Some of those moments will be from last week, last month, or last year. And some of those moments are in need of redemption from long ago. It is important to *understand* that when we are Moment Takers and not Moment Makers, we rob someone else of their moment and we at least need to try and redeem it.

Greer, you may write me back today. You may never write me back. But if and when you do, I can only pray that you will allow me to redeem that moment and maybe, just maybe, meet you back on the top of Rehoboth Hill.

See you guys at the bottom ...

CHAPTER 11

RESCUING WEAKNESS

If Disneyland is supposed to be the happiest place on earth, why is it that every time I go there, 99 percent of the people seem miserable? Because it costs $3,334.43 to take your family of four, and you get to ride a total of three rides after waiting in lines for hours in ninety-eight-degree weather. Yeah, *that* makes sense. Still, knowing this, day after day people pile into cars and unpile into a kingdom that promises them joy and happiness.

And somehow even at our most miserable, when we can dress up in a little happiness, it has the power to cleanse our moods, our hearts, and our minds. You know what I mean? All the lines, all the sweat, all the crying—it all goes away when your four-year-old princess dances a fifteen-second waltz with Cinderella. It all goes away when you feel your gut leave you on the drop of Space Mountain. It all goes away when you get to the front of the hot dog line, they swipe your debit card, and it still gets approved three meals later. Those moments ... that is happiness ...

In spite of knowing that the ever-smiling Pooh is actually a miserable 4'11" teenager from Compton and Minnie Mouse is actually a 4'8" thirty-six-year-old, chain-smoking Vietnamese immigrant living in Buena Park. Oh. You didn't know that? I apologize. How would I know this you ask? Well, because *I* was Eeyore.

Back in the spring of 1998 I was an undergraduate at California Baptist University. Tucked in the smog-ridden valley of the San Bernardino mountains was a college where lots of young Baptists hung out doing Baptist things on a daily basis. You know, like smuggling beer into their rooms past the RA and sneaking in and out of the rooms of members of the opposite sex after hours.

And learning the meaning of God's grace the next day after sneaking out of the room.

Driving back home to your dad's church every weekend because you were also the youth minister. Typical Baptist college.

I was new at school after failing out of Berry College. Although, failing out seems like such a weak way to explain how I exited Berry College. It was almost the opposite of failing because it felt like winning to me! It was grand.

When I first landed at California Baptist University I felt a bit out of place.

I was twenty-three and dead-set on no one knowing I was the old guy who failed out of his last school and had to have his daddy call in several favors to help him get into the school where he served on the board of trustees. In a matter of weeks I went from partying with rednecks to hanging with *cholos*. And in the same head-spinning disruption to my world, I went from spending Daddy's money partying at school to being completely cut off and needing to find a job ASAP. So I started pounding the pavement.

I spent an entire afternoon at Tyler Mall gathering applications, and when I got home I had pretty much determined I would drop out of college and become homeless before I would ever work at the mall. All of the on-campus jobs paid peanuts, and I wasn't about to file papers for the mean old lady in the school of education and human sciences. Even though I didn't know it at the time, I needed a Moment-Making job.

Early one Tuesday morning I was walking past the campus theater when I saw the flyer: "Disney Character Auditions. Saturday Morning 7:00 a.m., Disneyland Campus, Anaheim." Disney character auditions? Like Mickey Mouse? I am totally going to quit school and become Tigger!

Saturday morning could not come fast enough. On Friday night I asked my buddy Mark if he wanted to go with me, and he responded with: "Dude. Seriously? You *want* to do that?" I took that as a no and set my alarm for 6:00 a.m.

I woke up earlier than I had in years because I was certain that this would be the day I would become Tigger. I walked out the door dressed in my Adidas soccer shorts and my intramural basketball T-Shirt and started my drive down the 91 toward the OC. On the drive down I remember the sun rising over the mountains of Santa Ana to my left, and, for the first time since I set out on this adventure, the thought occurred to me ... "I wonder if you need some special skills other than being awesome to pull this off?"

Soon after pulling into the Disneyland employee parking lot, my question was answered. First of all, there were not a few dozen people who showed up to this audition ... there were hundreds. Seriously, that's not an exaggeration. I counted. And all of them were very skinny, very flexible dancer-looking types. All the guys had shirts with "CATS" written across them or some other Broadway-ish logo to make sure you knew they were very performance-abled dudes, while all the girls had "Flash Dance"-style cut up sweatshirts.

I was a semi-overweight Mexican lad who couldn't touch his toes without bending his knees. The only dancing I had ever done was the breaking kind on a flattened cardboard box in Catherine Write's driveway ... and that was in fourth grade.

What had I gotten myself into?

They herded us into groups of twenty or so, and then we were left to wait.

"Hey, man. I'm Carlos. Have you done this before?" I asked one of the really limber dudes in my group. "Oh, honey, yes. This is my fourth time auditioning. Most of us are back for another round of rejections. You definitely seem like a Disney audition virgin. Are those Umbros you have on?"

That's when I knew ... I was on the freeway toward inadequacy, and this back-lot Disney dance hall was my El Camino. When my group was finally called into the room full of mirrors and hardwood floors I knew I was in deeeeeeeeep trouble.

Every guy in the room started stretching and bending and hiking their legs up onto wooden poles attached to the mirrors that ran horizontal to the floor.

The only way this could turn any worse was if those poles were attached vertically — floor to ceiling — and well, you know ...

"Okay, guys!" a very bendy and very loud man announced from the front of the room.

"It goes like this ... five, six, seven, eight ..."

And he was off.

Ninety seconds of dancing complete with snapping fingers and spinning on the balls of your feet. My chin dropped to the floor. The deal was he would show us the dance only three times, and then we were supposed to pull it off just as he did.

I tried. I desperately tried. But my legs and mind were having no part of it. By the third run-through I had become a bit of a distraction for the rest of the guys in my group. When they went left I went right. When they crouching-tigered, I hidden-dragoned. It was a hot mess.

"Hey, man. If you can't take this seriously, then just leave," one of the "real" dancers yelled at me. And then it hit me. When you can't be as good as they are at their game, make up your own. Let me say this again ... clearer: There will be moments — big moments — in life when you realize that you're in over your head.

But those are precisely the moments where you *do not* pack your bags and head home.

No. Those are the moments when you dig in your heels, the moments when you fight to stay in the game. Break the established rules and create your own set of rules. The worst thing that could happen is that you fail. And, well, at this point, there is already a strong chance of failure. So why not break the rules and have some fun while you are at it? Chances are, the new rules you are creating are more likely to deliver you victory in that moment than if you didn't try at all.

And this launched the upward trajectory of my day. When it came time to do the dance I hung on tight for the first fifteen seconds ... And then I reverted back to my fourth grade cardboard-wearing-out self. It began with the worm, and by the time we hit forty-five seconds I was already on my third backspin. The really serious guys in my group were horrified. I ended with "The Dirty Bird" and even took a bow when the music ended. Everyone was completely stunned. I'm sure they were looking for hidden cameras. If looks could kill, I would have been killed twenty-three times.

"Okay. If we call your number, you will move on to the next phase of the audition. If we don't call your number, please consider auditioning again in the spring." Ninety seconds later ... "453!" Umm. That was me. I picked up my backpack and walked to the hallway where we were ushered into another room.

At this point, the over six hundred people in the first round had been sliced down to about 120. Then came more dancing ... Three hours later. Now, there were twenty-six of us. I'm still there. "Okay, ladies and gents. Mrs. Humbolt will now come in and measure you for a costume and you will have to do the dance you completed in round one. But this time wearing full Disney costumes."

When you are a Moment Maker, there will be moments that come by that make you think: "This is it. There is never going to be another day I will experience something like this." And the moment I walked into that dance hall and looked into the floor-to-ceiling mirror only to see Brer Fox staring back at me was one of those moments.

I was certain that by the time they made their cut down to the fourteen they were keeping for this job, I wouldn't be one of them. But I was also certain that I would never forget this mirror moment for the rest of my life.

I was Brer Fox.

And I was about to break dance in that costume.

Two hours, three interviews, and three dances later I found myself in the employee parking lot of Disneyland on the phone with my girlfriend (now my wife), Heather.

"I made it! I'm a Disney character."

"Um. Congrats baby. But if you plan on a future with me, I'll just tell you right now, I'm not marrying Eeyore."

Those words would haunt the beautiful Heather the rest of her life.

Three days later we had to go in for the formal costume fitting.

Remember: Mrs. Humbolt was the official costume fitter for all of Disneyland.

Every single character to grace the streets of this Disney park had to pass Mrs. Humbolt's test. She was responsible for making sure there were no discrepancies from venue to venue and that the integrity of the character costume remained the same through the years.

So ... Tigger. Remember Tigger? That was the goal. When they finished taking my measurements and I walked out of the costume room, I was handed the slip of paper with my character assignments on it. Eeyore and Tweedle Dee. *Eeyore and Tweedle Dee!*

A depressed donkey and a really frightening man with obvious mental issues. This was what eight hours in a dance audition had brought me. A far cry from Tigger.

I'm going to give you, the reader, just a moment to pull up your favorite web browser on whatever device you have handy and search for this: Tweedle Dee Disneyland; then search for this: Eeyore Disneyland. Notice the similarities in the costumes—specifically, in the midsection. Yes, my friends. This was the Disney fate of the fat guy.

I was told that if I lost about thirty pounds she would assign me different costumes, but for now these were the costumes that fit my body type. *Umm. Excuse me?*

I could have spent a lot of time feeling offended, but I needed the job, and as it turned out, I had a lot of fun and made a bunch of moments that year.

Seeing huge smiles from the park visitors through the eyes of their cartoon friends was amazing.

That moment when I knew that I was screwed but had to go through with it anyway—the moment in the dance hall when Carlitos was asked to do a dance he'd never seen with a bunch of guys who were trained for it—that moment.

That was when I rewrote the rules in order to save the moment. I used my weakness to show God's strength. Not with a megaphone, but with a dance move.

The path to becoming a Moment Maker is going to be full of circumstances when you will find yourself in way over your head, times when you will find yourself in need of a miracle in order to pull off the impossible.

I love this quote by Ralph Waldo Emerson: "Do not follow where the path may lead. Go instead where there is no path and leave a trail."

Fellow Moment Makers, the path that day was set for me to stumble and fall on the trail toward a perfect dance. That was the path set before me.

In that moment I could have tried to learn a dance, failed at a dance, and gone home frustrated like all of the really flexible guys who had auditioned over and over. But knowing what was in front of me and that I had little hope of succeeding in it, I changed the rules. The choice that day, and all the way to this point in my life, is the same. Blaze a trail.

I knew what my skill set was. And I was really clear on what it was *not*.

I knew there was no way I would outmaneuver this bunch of really flexible dudes in a room full of mirrors. You know your own limitations. You see, friends, only you can blaze your own trail. You can do that every single day. And along that path you create you will experience miracle moments like you would never imagine.

Later on during the day of my audition, one of the character managers came up to me and said, "We knew you couldn't pull off that dance. But watching you own that truth made us put you through to the next round. Don't stop doing that. Don't stop taking risks or changing who you are."

I didn't really know what that meant as a young lad in Umbro shorts.

But my oh my does it make sense now. Where was *So You Think You Can Dance* back then? I could have been a big star.

There are things we want to do. Moments we want to make. But we have a tendency to get in our own way.

There is an important message I need you to hear. We all have limitations. We all have fears. But Jesus meets us right where we are and guides us through the steps to overcoming them. Look at Saul. He was killing Christians, angry, and disillusioned. He felt threatened. So he lashed out. Jesus stopped him in his tracks on the road and called him out.

There he was on the road to Damascus. I'm sure it was already a miserable hike. But Saul was probably high on the energy of his radical rebellion against anything good. So as Jesus often does with so many of us, he stopped Saul in his tracks. And I don't mean stopped him by maybe a donkey traffic jam or a boulder in the middle of the road. No. He does it the way God would do it. He blinds Saul. Blinds him. No way outta this one Saul. You can't see.

A bright light. Saul falls to the ground, and before Saul can even get a sound out, God speaks first. "Saul, Saul, why do you persecute me?" What I find amazing here is that God speaks first. He doesn't wait for Saul to figure out what is going on. It's a loud reminder to me that sometimes when life knocks us down, we should probably just lie there a minute before we get up and see if we hear anything like Saul did.

Then Saul responds, "Who are you, Lord?" First Saul asks who are you, and then he followed that by calling him Lord. Ignore my lack of seminary training for a moment because I think Saul answers his own question here. Who else is gonna blind you and then speak from the sky?

And so the Lord replies, "I am Jesus, whom you are persecuting."

Jesus. But he didn't stop there. He didn't stop at simply blinding a murderer. No. He called him to a higher purpose. Saul became Paul and began to walk the streets preaching anywhere he could, telling of this man named Jesus who was the son of God.

Take a moment to look at the goals we have and how we may be inadequate for the dreams at hand. For me it was the dream of dancing like Aladdin yet never taking one second of dance in my life. Small dream I know. But my inadequacies proved just the thing that pushed me over the top. For you it may be wanting to be a teacher but lacking the schooling to get a job. For others it may be wanting to run a marathon but you haven't walked farther than the sofa to the mailbox in years.

Those things may seem insurmountable, but remember *Saul was killing Christians*. He stopped at a synagogue and the people literally said, "Isn't he the man who raised havoc in Jerusalem among those who call on this name? And hasn't he come here to take them as prisoners to the chief priests?"

Nobody could believe that this guy is now a follower of Christ. I mean even the disciples themselves couldn't believe it. According to Acts 9, when Saul got to Jerusalem he tried to join the disciples and they were all like, "Nope. Thanks, but no thanks, man. We know who you are." That's a Carlos paraphrase but you see where I'm coming from. And who could blame them?

Saul became Paul and reinvented himself, but it wasn't just a new identity. It was a heart change. I got a new identity in that audition, in that costume, that helped me realize I wasn't just a kid playing dress-up. When the character department finally let me put on that costume, they could no longer tell if I was a guy wearing a CATS shirt and leotards or this kid who's never danced a day in his life. And with that new identity I suddenly began to act like I belonged and believed. When I began to act like I was a Disney character, I became a Disney character.

The same thing can happen for you when you embrace your weakness in the moment and allow Christ to redefine you. If you want to be a teacher, then when you encounter a moment when you have an opportunity to teach, go ahead and teach. If you want to run a marathon, in the moment you walk from the sofa to the mailbox, do it twice. All it takes is that moment of decision where you allow Christ to be the one who defines your ability, not you. Because we know all things are possible through Christ alone. He *wants* you to start blazing that trail. What is the moment you are up against, knowing you are in over your head?

Are you going to turn around? No.

Are you going to sit and wait for it to open up for you? No.

Are you going to pull out your machete and start trail blazing? *Yes!*

Use your weakness to show his strength. *Live*, Moment Makers. It's time to trail blaze! Rescue the moment by showing how your inadequacies lead to your strengths. Break the rules set before you. Now go. Blaze.

CHAPTER 12

RESCUING SILENCE

Butterflies. Free. Wind. Glide. Flutter. Beauty. Spirit. Flow. Color. But pluck the wings off one of those bad boys and all you have left is a nasty-looking bug that you would step on in a heartbeat if it crawled close to your picnic lunch. It's amazing what a set of wings will do, huh?

When my daughters were old enough to realize that they were at risk of being the last of their friends to get a pet, I did what any reasonable dad would do. The conversation went something like this:

"Daddy, the Bergstroms have a dog. The Smiths have a dog. The Wilsons have a dog."

"Baby, we are not the Bergstroms, Smiths, or Wilsons."

(Now, why I said that I will never know. I *hated* it when my parents would say that to me.)

"But you know what, kids? We need to see if you can take care of an animal before we even begin to talk about owning one. Your mom has an idea ..."

Notice how I did that? Already anticipating this not going well, I placed the blame directly on the mother.

We went to Amazon.com and ordered a Butterfly Farm. Not

only was this an amazing father getting his kids a "pet," he is getting them an entire *farm*! Dad of the Year!

My daughters were over the moon, but I know the ugly truth about these creepy bugs in disguise. A few years ago, I walked into a butterfly farm at some botanical garden in England and about had a nervous breakdown as these winged, hairy monsters with eyes assaulted me from every direction. I was dive-bombed from every angle as they tried to use me for a landing strip. But rather than spoil the surprise, I decided I would let my kids figure all this out on their own.

Now, understand this "farm" we ordered was more like a mesh cage the size of a large Elmo doll and not like the dark, hot, humid room where I was attacked by these creatures like the ending of *Men in Black*.

Let me let you in on the fact that my kids are total animal lovers. Especially my nine-year-old. If we should happen to pass PetSmart on a Saturday morning while they have their Adopt-A-Pet sidewalk events, she will inevitably begin crying over how bad the dogs must "feel." I did not know that this would translate from the mammal family to the Lepidoptera family. But it did.

The morning the "farm" arrived was full of disappointment. I'm sure that when we told them they were getting a butterfly farm they anticipated much greater things. When they saw the box they said, "How is a farm in there, Daddy?"

But they were not to be discouraged. They started their little farm with four caterpillars. They were cute in a nasty sort of way. Worming around that little mesh cage looking like every elementary school recess black top in 1984. It was marvelous. After a week or so they slowly made their way to the top of the mesh cage and began the process of encasing themselves in their worm saliva and liquefying their little worm bodies until somehow this equals birth and beauty on the other end. Keep in mind, this all took place in my kitchen.

So every morning as I made my cup of coffee I would look on the counter, and there they were: Billy, Jordan, Misty, and Sam. After a week they were somehow part of the family. My kids actually knew how to tell them apart. They were butterflies for a good week before it was time to let them go. And if you know anything about the Whittakers, it is that we don't do anything halfway. Go big or go home.

We woke up the Sunday morning of "Release Day" to butterfly pancakes, antenna headbands, and coloring pages to depict the wondrous spectrum of colors on the wings of our soon-to-be-free friends. Giggles. Laughter. Joy. Colors. Joy. Pancakes. We made the pancakes in the shapes of butterflies. The kids wore little antenna headgear and wings on their backs to feel like butterflies. We painted butterflies on their cheeks. We were gonna make this a moment if it was the last thing we did. The stage was set. Epicness was ensuing ...

I mean there could be no better way to get ready for church. With fifteen minutes remaining before we had to leave for church we decided to get the festivities underway. Billy, Jordan, Misty, and Sam ... it's time to introduce you to the beauty of Nashville.

The kids had spent hours staring into the mesh cage, talking with these insects. They told them to behave and let them crawl onto their bony little fingers.

I was impressed. Our little farm had actually produced the happiness I had imagined. The family was on cloud nine.

We gathered around the cage; and Losiah, the six-year-old, picked it up; and we headed outside.

"Sohaila. Do you want to say anything?" I asked my seven-year-old. Tears filled her eyes. Tears of happiness mixed with despair. I knew she was sad to let them go but happy they would be free.

"No, Daddy. I just love them," she whimpered.

"Oh, baby. I'm sure they love you too." I lied.

Zzzzzzzzzzzzzip. Losiah unzipped the mesh door, and they were moments away from tasting what real flight was. *Fly, friends fly!* I swear it was like a scene out of some psychedelic hippy trip. Puffy clouds. Flying butterflies. Spinning children. Giggles. Pictures. All we needed was a rainbow in the sky. It was actually a quite amazing moment. There was something almost magical about watching these things go free.

"Okay, kids! Say bye to your butterflies! Wish them a good life. You have been good parents to them. They are free now, and it's time to head to church."

"Okay, Daddy," they politely replied. Dang. This morning has made angels out of my little sinners.

We climbed in. Buckled up. And started backing out. The kids had their faces pressed against the car windows looking for any sign of their winged friends. "Look, Daddy! There's one!" I looked in the rearview mirror and saw it on the right side. Fluttering around like a newborn baby calf trying to stand up. That thing had a few more hours of flying to do before it could fly like the Monarch she truly was. Then ... it happened.

As I started backing out, I looked over my right shoulder and saw it. Faster than Usain Bolt on his best day. It was more of a blur than anything. But this blur had purpose. This blur had a beak.

Even though she was a good fifty yards away, there was no time to distract the kids. No time to shield the horror I knew was coming. I swung my head around to scream at the kids to look at me. I had barely gotten the *H* out of "Hey, kids!" when she hit. That bird came out of nowhere, and right before my children's eyes, their faces smashed against the window like kids at the zoo ...

Misty the butterfly met her Maker.

The sound that escaped the seven-year-old's lungs was something out of a horror movie. It was low on the octave register and filled with saliva and strain.

"Daaaaaaaaaaaaaaaddddddyyyyyyyy!"

"The bird! The bird! She ate the butterfly!"

"Aghhhhhhhh! Go get it!"

Go get it? Like … chase the bird down? Of course. Chase the bird down, Carlos. I looked over to my right, and the wife was giving me *the look*. The look that said, "Are you just going to sit there while this bird destroys my children's lives?" So out I sprang.

The robin was in the middle of the street. Ticking her head side to side and pecking that butterfly on the ground into a most certain death. Sprint. Sprint. Scream. Sprint. *"Hey, bird! Hey, bird! Let the butterfly go!"* Did I really think I had a shot? No. Yet I got to within a foot of that chick before she took off. I'm fast. Misty was hanging from her beak. Over the house and away they went.

The walk back to the car was slow. I was trying to come up with something to say. Nothing I could think of worked.

Five minutes later we were heading down Interstate 40-E …

This was a funeral procession for sure. Filled with the wailing of souls left on earth mourning souls leaving for eternity.

"You know, kids. It's kinda like *The Lion King. Hakuna matata.* It's the circle of life!" I said.

"Hakuna matata means 'no worries,' Daddy! Not circle of life! *Wahhhhhhhh wahhhhhh!* Our butterfly is *not hakuna matata. She is not hakuna matata!"*

That didn't work.

"Kids! Maybe that birdie—" I used the term *birdie* to make the ferocious butterfly-eating monster seem less monstrous—"hadn't eaten in *days*! And maybe she was *sooo* hungry and needed to eat *sooo* badly that God let you raise the butterfly so the birdie wouldn't be hungry!"

"Wahhhhhhhhhhhhhhhh!"

"Wahhhhhhhhhhhhhhhh!"

"It never had a chance at life! *Wahhhhhhhhhh!"*

I looked to Heather … She looked back, and the look said it all. We got to church, prayed for the butterfly's soul, and sent our kids to endure a morning of singing and dancing about God, while they knew the truth about God now ... that the birds and the people he created don't always protect the innocent.

Later that afternoon I sat down next to the seven-year-old on the sofa.

She was still down.

"Baby? Are you still sad?"

"Yes, Daddy. I'm still sad," she replied.

"Come here, baby."

She put her head on my chest. And for twenty minutes or so I just held her.

I rubbed her tear-stained cheeks with my thumb and brushed her tear-soaked hair behind her ear. I just held her. She just cried.

As I was holding her, hearing her breathing slow and her heartbeat settle, I thought back to the moment in the yard and then the moment in the car. We had planned on that moment for weeks. The moment in the yard was filled with wonder and awe. It was a Created Moment that worked out better than we had hoped. We had no idea that this moment would need rescue. But then, we never do.

When the moment went horribly awry, I attempted to rescue it with what I thought was the best thing in my arsenal. Words. Not only was it *not* rescued by my words, it was beaten to a pulp by my words. No, the rescue was actually beginning now.

On this sofa, with my T-shirt soaking wet with my daughter's tears — this was the rescue. The rescue was beginning in the silence and truth of her reality. One soul holding another. The pain of this moment wasn't going to go away in a moment. The rescue was going to take time. The rescue was going to take an ear, a heart, and a chest to cry on. Words could come later, but in the beginning, it is a simple ear pressed to a heartbeat and allowing for the truth of her emotions.

* * *

Here is the application for us: *The rescue begins with under-standing.*

Think about any great rescue. Before anything can be rescued, everyone must agree to the truth of the situation and the person in need of rescue must see and believe the truth of their need. To understand is the greatest need. And sometimes the rescuer needs to understand more than those in need of rescue.

Jesus was the best at this. Let's look at what I consider one of the greatest rescues of all time. And one of the greatest shifts in understanding. It involves a man named Jairus. (The story can be found in Mark 5 and Luke 8.)

Jairus sprinted out of his house. His baby girl was dying. She was twelve and on death's door. She needed a healing. So her daddy ran as fast as he could to the only one he knew who could heal. Sprinting through the city, he finds Jesus surrounded by others in need of more and begs him, "My little daughter is dying. Please come and put your hands on her so that she will be healed and live." His heart was racing. It was in his chest. Pounding I'm sure. Out of breath. Hoping. Begging. Praying?

The crowd grew bigger as Jairus directed Jesus through the streets. They could not get home fast enough. Then the crowd swallowed up Jesus completely. A woman touched the fabric of Jesus and he stopped. "Who touched me?" Jairus was probably begging Jesus. Please hurry. But Jesus finished when the woman had revealed herself, "Daughter, your faith has healed you. Go in peace and be freed from your suffering."

Had this woman stolen his daughter's healing? Jairus ran off again. Pleading for Jesus to follow. They had lost valuable time. Yet I have come to the conclusion that Jesus could see Jairus out of the corner of his eye and knew exactly what Jairus needed.

Pushing. Begging. Running. Jairus and Jesus barely left the crowd when Jairus saw some friends. With despair and sadness in their faces, Jairus knew before they opened their mouths. "Your daughter is dead," they said. "Why bother the teacher anymore?" They were too late. It had taken too long. It was over. Her healing was not going to happen. But ...

Her resurrection was just beginning. God had much bigger plans for Jairus and his daughter. Much bigger than Jairus's understanding. When they got to Jairus's house, Jesus looked at the girl and said, "Little girl, I say to you, get up!" And she got up. *She got up!* Jairus was hoping for a healing. What he got instead was a resurrection.

Some of us have friends who are in need of rescue. Some of us ourselves are in need of rescue. So what I pray for is *understanding*. If we are too focused on words and actions, we can miss the real answer. When we tell God how to handle a situation, we limit the possibilities. It is important to attempt a rescue, but we *must* seek understanding first.

We hope for healing in so many areas of our lives. When Jesus wants to give us something so much bigger. Complete death of our old selves, pains, relationships, and fears. He doesn't want to heal you. He wants to resurrect you.

CHAPTER 13

RESCUING FEELINGS

Sixteen years old. My Afro parted precisely down the left side of my dome. A buck-forty-five soaking wet. Most amazing acid washed jeans perfectly ironed and pinch rolled. "Knights of the Round Table" shirt buttoned to the neck. ("Knights of the Round Table" was a knock-off version of Polo, and they had the same little guy on a horse except the pole he was holding had a little flag at the end of it. I became very skilled with a needle and attacked that flag like a surgeon, and within fifteen minutes of my mom bringing home a new Knights shirt, I had turned that Kmart copy into a fake Polo that would fool most people.) Drakkar down my neck. Eleven real roses and one silk rose in hand—because, just like the one silk rose, my love for April Veras would never die.

I was ready. Or so I thought.

A day earlier I had walked up to my dad. "Dad. I think I'm ready to date," I said.

"You *think*, son?" he said.

"Umm. I mean, I *am* ready."

"Carlos, come here. Sit with me."

Dear God, please do not let this be Birds and Bees, Part Two.

I sat.

(Read this next paragraph with the accent of "The Most Interesting Man In The World" — 'cause that's exactly what my dad sounds like.)

"Her name was Isabella," he said. "She was the most beautiful girl in all of Panama. I cried for days because she broke my heart. Yes, me. Your father. I wept and wailed. I stayed in bed for days. For she was the most beautiful creation the Lord had ever made. And she was gone, Carlos. Isabella wasn't mine. She never was. Your mother was and is. But I did not know this yet. This girl. April. She is somebody's wife, and you will someday be somebody's husband. You guys go have fun. But remember that she doesn't own your heart. God does. Oh, and I own your butt if you touch her, okay?"

With that he handed me forty bucks and the spare car key. And so it began.

If there is anything that you guys have figured out in this book it's this: I had a bad habit of tossing my heart into the air like a clay pigeon on a shooting range, and countless high school girls took aim and smoked it.

April was different, though. She was kind. She was focused. She said yes. Yeah, she said yes to going out. This increased the chances I would fall in love with her by approximately 400 percent. I mean, it wasn't like I was asking girls out on a regular basis. It's just that when I did, most of them gave me the "Sorry, I have a boyfriend" excuse, which also confirmed I did not have the persuasion skills to make it as an FBI agent.

The day of the date I was a disaster. I was nervous. I couldn't concentrate. I wanted to throw up. This could have something to do with it being my first date. It also could have had something to do with how beautiful April was. I was beyond nervous. The hours crept closer. And suddenly, as the hour was upon me, I was faced with a decision. The sort of decision that any sixteen-year-old male going on his first date is forced to make. It was a defining moment for the next two years of my life. And it played out like this ...

I honestly think I just drove to his house and knocked on the door.

It is all a blur—all except for the conversation.

"Andy. What are the chances you can hang out in my trunk for a few hours? Well, not really a few hours. Just like thirty minutes, then you can get out until we get back in the car after dinner and a movie? I think just knowing you were there would calm me down a bit."

"Sure, Los. Let me go grab a flashlight," Andy responded.

Sure, Los. *Sure, Los?* In the moment, I obviously wasn't surprised because I was the one who asked him. But looking back I now know one thing: I suck at friendship. Or Andy was the best at it. Because ninety seconds later he walked out of his house with a flashlight, three *National Geographic* magazines, and a pillow.

He climbed in the trunk and looked at me before I shut it ...

"What time am I free to get out?" he asked.

"Well, I'll be picking her up in five minutes, and I have dinner reservations at Red Lobster in twenty-five minutes. So just wait five minutes after you hear us get out of the car. Okay?"

Andy asked, "What time do I get back in?"

I replied, "*Sister Act* gets out at 7:45. For the love of all things holy, please be back in the trunk by 7:35. That will give us some margin for error."

Margin for error?

I showed Andy how to pop the backseat down and climb into the driver's seat. I immediately put in my new *Straight Outta Compton* cassette and started reciting every line so that, you know, I could psych myself up before I walked in and saw April.

"It's too loud back here!"

Oops. I turned it down. I was at April's in less than five minutes.

"Okay, Andy. You have the plan right?"

"Got it, man. You got this. Go get the girl."

And with that, I got out of my dad's Honda Accord with the pop-up lights I thought were the jam and walked to the door. Knock, knock, knock. Roger answered. *Roger answered.* Roger Veras was my hero. He was the captain of the varsity soccer team. He was dating Janet, the captain of the cheerleading team. He had never spoken a word to me.

"Umm. Hey, man. Umm. Is ... um ..."

"April! Carlos is here!" he yelled back into the house.

He knew my name. He said my name. Roger Veras said my name.

"Come in, man. How's it going? Are you gonna try out for varsity this year? 'Cause you totally should." Was I dreaming?

And then I knew I was, because April floated down the stairs looking more brilliant than the sun settling in for sleep across the Pacific. I think my mouth actually may have fallen open. She was radiant.

"Just keep your hands to yourself, buddy," Roger reminded me with a smile.

"Umm. Yeah. Totally. My dad told me the same thing," I replied. *What! Did I just say that?*

"Roger. Stop embarrassing me! And, Carlos, let's go to the movie!" April said.

With that she grabbed my hand, and out the door we went. The second she touched my hand all nervousness left. The hot mess of a Latino I was only minutes earlier had morphed into Antonio Banderas on his best '90s day. We walked out the door and turned toward the car. And then I remembered ... there was a human being in my trunk. What was I thinking? *Oh, dear God, forgive me.*

April and I laughed the entire way to Northlake Village, which was one of the nicer strip malls in town. It had a Red Lobster *and* an AMC Cinema on site.

Sixty minutes, a dozen fried shrimp, six hush puppies, and twenty dollars later, we walked out of Red Lobster full of food and full of love. The date couldn't have been going any more smoothly.

As we walked from Red Lobster to the movie theater, I glanced left and saw my car. The backseat was down. The windows were all rolled down. And Garth Brooks was pumping from the stereo system. Andy was reclined halfway in the passenger seat and his legs were kicked up on the dash.

Seriously, if you needed a stock image of a happy teen in the mid '90s, this was your shot. I dropped the hands-to-yourself warnings and immediately placed my arm around April in an attempt to shield her view of the car and my monumental mistake in judgment. She immediately put her arm around me, and we proceeded to walk one hundred yards, arm in arm, just like those couples you all make fun of.

I'm sure *Sister Act* was an amazing movie. I'm sure it was one for the books. But I had no idea at the time, because all I could think about was Andy relaxing in my car. Andy was that friend who could fall asleep anywhere. And I knew, I just knew, that we were going to walk outside and find Andy asleep in the exact position I saw him in earlier.

Movie over. The walk begins.

When we walked out of the theater it was dark — dark enough that I couldn't quite see the car. As we got closer, I noticed Andy wasn't in the seat but all the windows were still down! April was chatting nonstop about the movie, and we were a good forty-five seconds from the car. I tried to pay attention but couldn't. Then I saw one window begin to slide up. Thirty seconds away. Another window up. And another. And finally, the last one. We were ten feet away when I saw the backseat flip up and latch shut. Mission Accomplished.

I dropped her off at home on time — without totally violating my promise not to touch her. "Thanks for dinner and the movie.

I'll see you in Spanish class tomorrow, Carrrrlos!" She awkwardly rolled her *r*'s, but it was okay. She melted me, and I knew the beginning of an amazing relationship had just been forged.

"Andy. You okay?" I yelled when I got back in the car.

"Yeah, man! So sorry about that close call. I fell asleep."

We got back to his house and dissected the date. I thanked him for being my security blanket and proceeded home.

"Dad. Thanks again for the car and the money. I think I'm in love." He laughed, muttered something in Spanish to my mom, and proceeded to change the channel to *Silver Spoons*.

I could end the story here and dive into an explanation of how sometimes we think we need more than just Jesus. I could compare Andy to some sort of coping mechanism or draw a parallel between April and what fun it is to have a relationship with Christ. But I can't ... for two reasons.

First, that is a horrible analogy.

And second ...

And second is that little did I know Andy was "in love" with Kelly. And Kelly happened to be April's best friend.

Remember the part about me making hasty decisions and not doing my research before taking action?

The next day I got to school, and the second I drove up, seven of the soccer players from the varsity team all popped their trunks at the same time. I walked to my locker. It was littered with pictures cut out of magazines of cars with their trunks open. It was over. Over before it even began. I had to wait till second period to see Andy. I didn't even say anything as I walked past his desk.

"Sorry, man," he whispered. "She promised she wouldn't tell." And with that statement I knew Andy had told Kelly who had told April who had told her brother who had told the soccer team. Who needs Twitter?

There was no rescuing this moment. None whatsoever. I thought as hard as I could to figure out a way out of this mess. It wasn't there. I tried my best to find some way to make it go away. I was at a loss. I did everything I could to come up with some idea for how to rescue this for me. I had nothin'.

Then I saw her. She walked past me in the hallway. Her eyes were red — swollen from the tears that had been falling from them for hours, I'm sure. It was then that I realized the rescue that needed to occur wasn't just for me. I had thoroughly embarrassed not just myself, but this girl that I so wanted to impress.

She wouldn't talk to me, so I slipped her a note through one of her friends who obviously hated me with every inch of her Debbie Gibson looking self. "Fine. I'll give it to her. But she won't write back. So don't wait up." I didn't need a note back. I simply needed to rescue her out of a moment I had selfishly created.

* * *

Jesus reminded us in Matthew 5:23 – 24: "If you are offering your gift at the altar and there remember that your brother or sister has something against you, leave your gift there in front of the altar. First go and be reconciled to them; then come and offer your gift."

This passage demonstrates the importance of reconciliation. It is so high up there on the list of things we are supposed to do that God doesn't even want to hear from us until we have made things right with our fellow human beings if we have wronged them. The reason this is so critical is because we can't really connect with him honestly — or with anyone else — if we haven't acknowledged and tried to resolve issues that stand between us.

I had to make things right with April. I had apologized and tried to rescue her from the pain I had caused her. The moment of rescue had to do entirely with what she was experiencing in the aftermath of my carelessness. I thought I had dodged a bullet when the date went off without a hitch, but your sins still have a way of finding you out.

Dear April,

I'm so sorry for what I did. It was wrong. And I am also, quite obviously, insane. I think a lot of you and was super nervous. So that's all.

Thanks for reading,

Carlos

That's all it said. The more I wrote the crazier I sounded so I just stopped.

April and I never went on another date. Honestly, I didn't go on many more dates with any girls from Shamrock High the remainder of my time there.

But I did get a note back from April. Take that Debbie Gibson! It's been a while, but here is the gist of it.

Carlos,

Sorry we both feel it today. Thank you for the date.

April

Pretty epic, huh? Nope. But you know what that did for me? It showed me that all she wanted was acknowledgment—acknowledgment of the moment that everything went south. It was a needed *pause* in my Moment-Making journey to consider the possibility of collateral damage. At that point she could see my pain for what it was and the recovery began.

Began. Not *ended*. Big difference. So here's to first dates, bad ideas, and new perspectives.

CHAPTER 14

RESCUING OPPORTUNITIES

M oment Making is about writing the story of our lives. And the only way you can fully appreciate the significance of this particular moment is by reading a blog post I wrote nearly a decade ago right after my middle child was born. Here is the setup:

I am thirty. *Thirty.* Did you hear me? I am half way to sixty. I have a wife, two girls, and a cat named Riggins. I drive a Hyundai Santa Fe. I have been balding for nine years. People call me Pastor. I go to sleep before 10:00 p.m. and wake up around 6:30 a.m. Except for my small ears, there is no reflection of who I once was in me. But then again, I think that's a good thing.

How did I get here? Sin, love, move, love, move, sandals, guitar, Disneyland, marriage, consummation, baby, Camry, baby. That is about how it went down. And here I am. I have had a pounding headache for the last day that does not seem to want to go away. I wonder if it has to do with an eighteen-month-old and newborn screaming at the top of their little lungs at the same time? Funny how it always seems to happen in stereo. Stereo? Yup. Seanna (*say-AH-nuh*) Jess Whittaker. We have another one. Sixteen days old.

It seemed like a cool name until I realized that you can't really say both names in the same sentence without sounding like you are swearing in Arabic. But what were we supposed to name baby number two after Sohaila? We really couldn't go for Beth or Mary or Pam. So Seanna it is. I like it.

I know, I know. After Sohaila was born, it took me all of four days to write my thesis on Fatherhood and Labor. Not that the two are linked in any way. But this one took me sixteen days. I'm a little older and wiser now. Not to mention lazier as well. At least you are getting the scoop within the first month. Here's how it went down.

7:00 a.m. October 18, Saturday morning. Westin Hotel, San Diego

Here is a perfect example of the woman I married. Our due date is the seventeenth of October. That would be yesterday. And we are at a marriage retreat in San Diego. There is no fear in my wife. I have kind of learned just to go with the flow, and when things turn ugly, I'll step in. We spent the evening before in a few good seminars while everyone stared at me thinking: "I can't believe Carlos dragged his poor pregnant wife to this retreat! For God's sake! She is due today!" No one actually said anything, but if looks could kill . . .

Seven hours later I woke up to Heather and a stopwatch. It is Saturday morning. Labor has begun. She is having light contractions, but contractions nonetheless. My vote is let's get home so she can rest there. Once again I am overruled. She claims she is fine and reminded me that Sohaila took nearly two days of long, drawn-out labor, and she was not even in that much pain at the moment. So off to the sessions we went. Once again I got the stares from the people and smiled politely back. Little did they know I was the hostage here.

I found it rather humorous though that every five minutes or so Heather would tighten up and grimace for about thirty seconds and then continue taking notes on how I could be a better husband. When the seminars were over, we went to have lunch. Then went shopping at American Eagle and the

Gap. Finally, Heather said it was okay to head back to River-side. Thank God.

4:00 p.m. Riverside, CA

So, by now I am wondering what is going on here? Where was all the moaning and groaning? Maybe we were destined for a weeklong labor. Heather sent me to Papa John's for some grub. She and my mom stayed at the house with Sohai-la. Her contractions were getting a little stronger, but nothing relatively close to the first child. We thought this kid was still twenty or so hours away. As I normally do, I took a little longer than needed to get my errands done. I stopped by the of-fice; stopped by a buddy's apartment; bought a 64-oz. Cherry Coke Slurpee at 7–11; took the scenic route home ...

6:00 p.m.

I cruise back up my driveway and park in the garage. I walk in to a pretty peaceful scene—Grandma on the sofa with So-haila reading a book; The *Joe Schmo Show* recording on my TIVO. But there is no sign of Heather. I walk into the bedroom and find my wife panting on the bed "Hee hee hee hoooo." She is beginning to get that demented look on her face. The one I never want to see again. We both come to the conclu-sion that we won't go to the hospital because they will just send us home like they did with Sohaila. We will try to tough it out during the night.

Sohaila is not too hip on seeing and hearing Mommy in this much pain. But in our little two-bedroom home there is not much room to hide. So, around eight o'clock we decided to head out to Kaiser Permanente, knowing that the chances of being sent home were pretty big, but our house was get-ting smaller by the minute.

About a block away from home Heather is screaming for me to pull over. What? Okay. I pulled over. No questions. About one minute later we were off again. Two blocks later, *"Pull over!"* At this rate we will make it to Kaiser in twelve hours. So I simply stated that bit of information. *Wrong move.* My wife is not a cusser. She is quite the lady. But those rules seem to go out the window whenever labor is involved. She proceeded to fill me in on the amount of pain she was in and how I just needed to be quiet and obedient until this child comes out. (That was the edited version.)

I actually thought it was pretty cool to hear her swear like that. It reminds me that she was not raised in a Baptist minister's home as I was. Now she just lives with one. I was wondering why she was not able to sit down the whole way to the hospital. She was kind of in this half-stretched, stand up sideways position the whole way there. I thought this was weird. But only moments before I had learned not to state my opinion. So I just "thought" and did not speak. Well, after a few more stops and many inappropriate words later we arrived at the hospital. Our ten-minute ride was more like thirty minutes. But we made it. *Dear God, please let us be admitted so my epidural-loving wife could get her drugs. It would make my life that much easier.*

8:35 p.m.

We rolled into the parking lot, and I sprinted out to get a wheelchair. Heather was not going to get far on her little legs. She was really hurting now. I liken it to about hour twenty-four of labor with Sohaila. But even at this much pain they sent us home last time, so I was prepared.

Once again Heather flexed into that half-stretched, stand-up-sideways position as she boarded the wheelchair. She swore that she couldn't sit down. I wanted so badly to explain how it is one sits down. Place your behind on the seat and rest. I will then wheel you to a doctor. But, of course, I resisted, which meant it took us fifteen minutes to get to Labor and Delivery. Yeah. Fifteen minutes from the parking lot. We are talking about a two-minute walk. But the wheelchair express was sidelined every few minutes so she could "hee hee hee hoo." When we finally reached the third floor, I sensed something was different. Heather was absolutely delirious. I never saw her like this the first time. She was in pain, but never like this. She could barely move from her half-stretched, stand-up-sideways position.

As I was joking with the labor and delivery nurses, I heard a noise. It was like nothing I had ever heard before. Heather's voice dropped about six octaves. She sounded like Barry White on an acid trip. Seriously. Demonic sounding. "C A R L O S ... COME." At that very moment time stood still. The nurses all stopped in their tracks and looked at me like, "Did that just come out of your wife?!" All joking came to a screeching halt, and everyone went to work hooking my wife up to all the wires that beep and make me nervous.

9:00 p.m.

My wife is a stud. We all acknowledge that. She deals with life one day at a time and rarely, if ever, gets rattled. There is this book that we went over at the marriage retreat called *Men Are Like Waffles, Women Are Like Spaghetti*. Its premise is that men think in compartments—kinda like a waffle. We can only be in one box at a time. Our thoughts are focused. We have a TV box. A garage box. A computer box, etc. Women, on the other hand, are like spaghetti. Their thoughts and feelings flow together like noodles. They go from one concept, task, emotion, or responsibility to another without a second thought. Emotional spaghetti. The one thing I can say with certainty about Heather and me is that I am the emotional spaghetti and she is the focused waffle. We always do things backward.

All this to say: I am pretty much an emotional wreck right now. On the outside I look like the valiant husband looking out for his wife. On the inside I am jelly. Heather is strapped to this bed wailing that she wants to die. Me too, honey. The nurses are trying to calm her down. At this moment Heather has moved on to a new box in her waffle. It is called the epidural box. She looks at the midwife and begs her to admit us so she can get her epidural. I am begging as well. At Kaiser they do not admit you until you are dilated to three centimeters. You have the baby at ten centimeters.

With Sohaila we were at two centimeters for like twenty-four hours. So, you see my concern. Please tell me we are at least three centimeters so we can get admitted and give my wife some drugs, tequila, or anything numbing. Heather is all about not doing the natural thing. Some people claim you and your baby feel closer after a natural birth. Heather has no intention of feeling warm and snuggly during birth. Drugs. Drugs. Drugs. Since we have only been in mucho pain for about three hours, I am preparing for the worst—a long car ride home to "hee hee hee hoo" for a few more unbearable hours.

Our midwife checks Heather. She looks at me for a long second with a slight expression of concern on her face, and then smiles to let us know we will be admitted. That good news lasted all of three seconds. At least I got Heather to smile for a few seconds. Our friendly midwife went on to inform us that Heather is over nine centimeters dilated. "You're joking right?" I said. The nurse then shared with us that Sue, the midwife, does not joke about that stuff. Heather looked deep within Sue's eyes desperately and with her bottom lip outstretched spoke: "But what about my epidural?" *Bad news*. We missed the epidural window by a few hours. Sue looks back at Heather and informs her that this baby is coming out in a few minutes. Shoot. Heather went on to declare to the ward that she had no intention of delivering this baby without drugs. I wanted to tell her that gravity has more power than her mouth right now. She was having this baby naturally. No going back now.

Heather is the super-organized one. We had the call list to call people when we were admitted, when we had the baby, and when we got home. We had a bag for the waiting-room friends, full of board games, donuts, and magazines. We had a plan of attack for Sohaila and a babysitter to be called at all hours of the night. It was all planned. Heather's mom was in Pasadena. My mom was ten minutes away. Neither of them had enough time to make it before Seanna made her way into my world. All plans were spoiled. This kid wanted out.

9:15 p.m.

Heather wants to push, but the midwife tells her she has to wait a minute. Not knowing we were going to be having a baby so quickly, I left all the cameras in the car when we rushed into the hospital. Heather has enough energy to demand I run to the car and get the camera. The nurses warn that I will probably miss the birth if I leave for even five minutes. Heather cares not. She sends me out.

I sprint out to the Camry like the days when I was young and swift and make it back to the room as all the lights and doctors were asking Heather to push. Three pushes later ... I'm a father of two. As Heather's head slowly rotated back to its original position, I was compelled to spout out a few unnecessary hippie, granola, tree-hugger, natural-childbirth props out to my wife. I asked her if going natural was everything she had always dreamed of? Remember, I said she only cussed when in labor? Well, I take that back. Add ten minutes after labor to that.

9:30 p.m.

Seanna Jess Whittaker is my black baby. Sohaila came out white as a cloud. Seanna is representing Mexico well. Like an old Fat Boys lyric states, "One is black and the other is white, they never get in trouble and they never ever fight." Seanna is healthy and took to breastfeeding like white on rice. The moms made it and comforted my hero Heather. Her best friends made it and gave her some love. I just kept thinking how only hours earlier we were in San Diego shopping. Wow.

Sunday October 19, 10:00 a.m.

Twelve hours later we are home. Heather was ready to get back home. So home we went. I have to admit I was a bit worried about Sohaila. Eighteen months old is fairly young to bring another baby into her world. Seanna didn't stand a chance against the brute force I will simply refer to as Sohaila. Man was I wrong. If we take Seanna out of Sohaila's sight, Sohaila cries. If she is not in a place where she can touch her, she cries. If she has her in her lap, she is in heaven. *Thank you, Lord.*

It is funny how even though I wrote this nine years ago, I remember every sound and sight as if it were yesterday. Why? Well, obviously because it was the birth of my kid. That's number one.

But number two? That would be because I wrote it out. I wrote it out.

It took time. It took energy. It took focus. But because I spent the time to document, in my own words, this major moment in life, it remains so much more engraved than a picture or video could ever etch.

When we are making moments we are so quick to lift up our lenses that we don't realize we aren't fully participating in the moment. We don't realize we are losing what I believe may be almost half of the experience. We may feel we are capturing the moment when we click ... click ... but it's my belief that we are actually losing the essence of the moment.

God created our minds to be stronger carriers than Kodak could ever pull off. God created our mouths to paint the pictures of these stories in ways that a video could never collect. We are called to be Moment Makers. Not Moment Capturers. The capturing is happening for us in the way God beautifully engineered our minds to function.

Of course, I am not telling you to forget about your Instagrams and Pinterests. It is important to take photos and videos and other records of your life. But those photos only lead us back to the place where the stories are actually etched—in our minds and our hearts.

* * *

I look to Scripture and think sometimes, if Scripture was photographed and filmed, I think it would lose so much of its weight. We would miss so much that the Lord has allowed us to realize. There is power in the written word.

Heck. You are reading this right now. But I wrote it from my memory of the experience I had, not from the photo I took. And I promise you, no video could do justice to what happened that Saturday morning nine years ago.

Can you imagine if Jesus tried to pull out his iPhone to try to capture Peter walking on water? Peter would have drowned. "Wait one sec, Peter! Hold it right there! I've got to capture this moment!" Umm. No.

Or think about this one:

> As soon as Jesus was baptized, he went up out of the water. At that moment heaven was opened, and he saw the Spirit of God descending like a dove and alighting on him. And a voice from heaven said, "This is my Son, whom I love; with him I am well pleased." (Matthew 3:16–17)

Can you imagine if Jesus had asked God to hang on a minute before giving his speech so everyone could get a little video of the dove coming out of the sky and upload it to Facebook?

Jesus was too busy *being* the moment to have time to *capture* the moment.

When we *are* the moment, the moment becomes engrained in us. But when we are more concerned with having something to show for it, we miss out on the experience. We may have a photograph of our child's smile when they discover something new, but we didn't get to experience that discovery with them. When we are *in* the moment, the moment stays with us.

But when we're focused on documenting it, we lose the heart of what the moment is supposed to be. We may have a video of our beloved tearfully saying yes to our proposal, but if we were hidden behind a camera when that happened, we missed the connection that comes from looking deep into their eyes when they said, "I love you."

If there is anything at all you take away from reading these stories, I hope it is that life happens in moments and if we aren't paying attention and getting involved—if we aren't *living*—we will miss what they are really all about.

CHAPTER 15

RESCUING PATIENCE

It started as innocent as any Christmas tradition. But somehow Heather and I (okay, mostly I) figured out a way to traumatize our kids. That cute/creepy bug-eyed elf on every shelf at every Target store in America . . . I'd like to say it's his fault. But it's really mine. I'll explain in a second. But first, can we take a trip back to my third-grade year?

When I think back, I remember really needing only one tradition to make me happy during the Christmas season. Opening presents on Christmas morning!

Everything else my family threw at me was fluff. I remember making those popcorn strings that we wrapped around the tree. I remember going caroling. I remember having to sit on Santa's lap across from JC Penny's every year. It was the same crusty old man. And his breath was kicking something fierce. "Mom. Could we go to another mall this year?" I'd ask. Never giving away that Santa's breath was foul . . . just in case . . . you know . . . in case it really was him.

All those traditions. All those moments. They were nice and all. But bring on Christmas morning. Leave it to my generation to deliver a Christmas tradition that incorporated Christmas morning the entire Christmas season. How's that you ask?

Heather had been telling me about this Christmas tradition that our friends Stephanie and Mark were doing with their kids. It basically goes like this. Here is the *cute* part:

You buy your "Elf on a Shelf" kit, which comes with the elf and a book. Then you tell the kids that an elf has come from the North Pole into your house and asks your kids what they want for Christmas. (I mean, to me, that's a bit of a stretch from my understanding about how to get your message to Santa; but to each his own.)

Said elf then takes off every single night back to the North Pole to let Santa know what it is the kids want and makes sure the other elves are busy working on all of the presents.

The next morning said elf shows back up at your pad before the kids wake up and causes a bit of mischief in the house. *Cute!*

Ready for the *not so cute* (that is, *horrifying*) part?

This beady-eyed elf is supposed to spy on your kids and make sure he tells Santa absolutely every single naughty thing they do. And the eyes on this bad boy are *huge.* I swear they glow in the dark. But I figured I could look past the horrifying part for a second to create a moment for my kids.

I'm sold. Let's buy that junk. Now the burning question: How are we, the Whittakers, gonna take this up a notch? I knew how — by placing the smiling, beady-eyed elf outside our front door seated perfectly next to his book, then we'd knock on the door and sprint around to the back door to sneak in. Yeah, that's how.

Then the kids would think that the elf, with his tiny little felt hands, had some super elf strength that allowed him to pound on our front door. So that's what we did.

Knock, knock, knock, knock.

"What was that?" the five-year-old says.

"I don't know? Go check the door," I reply.

Nope. Not a chance. It's pitch black outside and something

just knocked on our door. She can see through the window on the door that no one is out there, and she's not about to open it. So the seven-year-old offers, "Daaaaad. I'll open it." Door opens ... this beady-eyed dude is sitting in front of it.

When I tried to look into his eyes and he never looked back, even I got a bit creeped out. I turned to the five-year-old ... she's petrified. I could see her mind spinning. The look was not just fear. The look was terror. I could tell that this was already—within forty-five seconds of the knock—going south fast. So I read her expression and tried to lighten the mood.

"Look! It's an elf from the North Pole! Maybe Santa sent him!"

I haven't mentioned the three-year-old yet—the only other male in the house. All boy. So he did what any normal non-elf-fearing toddler would do.

He walked directly to the front door and bent over with the intention of picking it up. He was stopped in his tracks.

"*Nnnnnoooooooooo!* He'll lose his magic powers!" the five-year-old screams.

Huh? Magic Powers?

"No, he won't, baby. Who told you that?" I said as I bent down to pick the elf up.

She was not having any of this. Whatever mechanism God places inside of your dome to tell you when to fight or when to fly was kicking in for Seanna. A stuffed elf who magically appears and knocks on the door harder than her daddy was not welcome in her home. And she was not at all happy about the current state of affairs.

We tried. Nothing. She was not having it. She was scared of it. And I don't blame her. Just look at it. Then she asked this:

"Is that a fiction elf?" she asked.

I looked over to Heather, and she was still now giving me the "Be Careful How You Answer This" look. I paused ... I paused some more ... I spoke cautiously ...

"Umm. Well. Baby. Don't worry. Sure. It may be a fiction elf. It may be a real elf. But we won't know until we read the book," I said. "Want to do that now, baby?" I whispered.

"Sure, Daddy," she replied in a tone that was less *Exorcism of Emily Rose* and more *Strawberry Shortcake*.

She was finally calming down.

I opened the book and started reading. She kept saying over and over that we had touched the elf and he's probably lost his magical power. Page after page there was nothing addressing this dilemma. But her relenting pressure was wearing on me. *Every* fifteen seconds while I was reading the book,

"Daddy! You touched the elf, Daddy! That's not good, Daddy. That's sooo ... sooo not good."

I'd finally had enough. I looked the five-year-old square in the eyes and said that was nonsense. Nothing we can do would take the elf's power away. So I thought I'd show her.

It all happened so fast. I don't even remember why I thought it was a good idea. But for some reason, I quickly grabbed the elf and slammed his head three times on the table.

"See, baby? He's just fine," I smiled.

Her eyes were as wide as the Atlantic. Heather's eyes were as well. Bad move. Move on quickly ...

As I continued reading the story, I explained how this elf— whom we are supposed to name—will fly to the North Pole every night and tell Santa what's up with the Whittaker kids. Then he will fly back every morning and the kids were supposed to find him.

Then I turned the page, and my mouth dropped, but not before I'd made the mistake of reading the following ...

"Do not touch me or I might lose my powers and not be able to fly to the North Pole and tell Santa all the nice things you are doing!"

Fantastic.

"*Seeeeee!* I told you! *Daddy! Waaaaahhhhhh!* Now we won't get anything for Christmas from Santa! *Waaaaahhhhhhhh!*"

The five-year-old was in hysterics. Not only is she freaked out that there is a bug-eyed, walking, knocking, and flying elf in her house; she is freaking out because her father murdered the elf right in front of her with three quick blows to the head. There was no rescue happening. This was over. Any attempt at salvaging the moment at this point would only serve to make things worse. That is ... until I saw the last page. It was my unexpected safety net.

On the last page there was a certificate with a place to write the elf's name, our family name, and the date.

"Baby! It's not official until we sign this! *Then* you can't touch him!"

I mean, c'mon, people. *Brilliant.* Talk about thinking on your toes!

So we all gathered around the certificate and started pitching names.

The kids quickly forgot about the attempted murder and were soon coming up with names like Elfie, Elfer, and Elfit. All horrible names, but I didn't care. The tears were over. We all grabbed the pen and started signing our names on the certificate. First went Mommy. Then I signed. Then the seven-year-old. Then the three-year-old. Then, finally, the five-year-old.

She looked up at me with her puppy dog eyes. She wanted to know if I was sure ... if I was sure that the head beating the elf took was not going to jeopardize this entire operation.

I promised I was sure.

She wanted to know what happened if a friend touched the elf. I said it only counted if one of our kids touched it. She wanted to know how the elf was going to get out of the house that night. I suggested, maybe up the chimney. She wanted to know if the elf would ever hide in her room.

I think she basically wanted to know if she was going to wake up at 5:00 a.m. to go potty and find that elf staring at her from above her bed. *Holy nightmares!*

After we signed the certificate, they reluctantly went upstairs and said goodnight to *Carlos*. Yeah, they finally decided that since I told them that their elf names needed some work, it would be my namesake.

A few minutes later, I grabbed the elf, hid it in my backpack, opened the door, and went upstairs.

"Who left the front door open?" I said.

The kids ran downstairs and saw the elf was gone.

"The elf is gone!" the girls yelled.

They tore throughout the house looking for him. He was gone. The relief on the five-year-old's face was nothing short of epic.

"See, kids. He didn't lose his powers! He's on his way back to the North Pole to tell Santa how amazing the Whittaker Family is!" I triumphantly exclaimed.

"But, Daddy," said the five-year-old, "you almost killed him. I don't think he will think that's amazing."

She doesn't miss much, does she? Hmm. Where did that parenting manual go?

* * *

We have been looking at various moments throughout my life where I attempted to rescue moments. None of them look even remotely like the other ones—the created and the received kind. So instead of looking for steps to follow when you are in a moment in need of a rescue, let's look for principles. The principle we need to land on here is that the rescue lies in which button to push. You basically have two options.

Let's imagine you are flying a plane. I know this is going to take tons of imagination because I know you probably don't know how to fly a plane. And if by chance you are a pilot, and you do know how to land a plane, please forgive the following illustration.

The first option is to Eject—hit the tiny red button under your

Moment-Making thumb. When you try to live a Moment-Making life, you will inevitably have moments you try to pull off that will fall apart in your face — surprise parties that weren't surprises; popping the Question and hearing no; planning an event for fifty-five people and five show up. It's okay to Eject. But I always keep that as the last resort.

The second option is to turn on Autopilot. The truth is that sometimes moments have a way of rescuing themselves without much intervention from you. Sometimes you just have to trust the process enough to have total trust that it's gonna land. And that is a scary thing. This is probably the scariest of the options because although moments often land themselves, if you are a control freak like I am, you either want to muscle the plane down yourself or bail out.

With the elf disaster I wanted to hit Eject. My thumb was on the Eject button for sure. I was preparing to eject but hoping I could bring it in for a landing. That landing was *so* bumpy that I realized I was out of control, found the Eject button, but hit Autopilot, and prayed.

I could have racked my head trying to rescue the elf moment for hours. In fact, I started making up some pretty convoluted stories to salvage the situation, and it only spiraled out of control. Luckily, the certificate saved me.

It is a great temptation to cut and run when things start going south. Jesus certainly could have done that in a moment that was going horribly wrong.

He was looking for an out when he went to pray in the garden:

"He went away a second time and prayed, 'My Father, if it is not possible for this cup to be taken away unless I drink it, may your will be done.'" (Matthew 26:42)

In fact, he had the mother of all Eject buttons. In Scripture Jesus lets us know that he has at his disposal more than twelve legions of angels. He says that not only can he call on his Father, but he has the alarm that sounds angel armies. Jesus could have ejected had he wanted to. But the Lord God himself chose to allow things to play out the way *we* needed them to—with us ultimately in charge and us ultimately putting him to death. We did that to him. He didn't hit Eject. But the opportunity was there. Instead, he went all in. He went to the death to make sure he could give us the greatest moment of our lives.

Moment Making is not for the weak at heart. Sometimes our moments crash and burn at the speed of a fighter jet plummeting toward earth in a fireball. At that velocity, sometimes there is nothing else you can do besides eject, but if you can hold on, sometimes you are presented with an even more incredible moment than what you thought was possible.

For some of you, your thumb is already hovering over that button. It may be a moment in a relationship. It may be a moment during an illness. It may be a moment during a business meeting.

Sometimes our moments start by hang gliding into a sunset . . . then we are hit by a hurricane we didn't see coming. When that happens it is okay to *eject*. If you find yourself in a situation when the potential for harm in trying to rescue a moment outweighs any benefit that might be had, eject. Live to create another moment.

But if you can, wait long enough to see what God may be doing in that moment that you have yet to understand. Just as Jesus's followers didn't *understand* in the moment why he had to leave them, why he had to die to save them, we may not know what lies on the other side of that moment that seems to be tanking. Sometimes, that's really how it was supposed to go all along.

THE MOMENT THAT MADE ME A MOMENT MAKER

Save us from these comforts.
Break us of our need for the familiar.
Spare us any joy that's not of You,
And we will worship You.

EIGHTEENTH-CENTURY PURITAN PRAYER

There is a numbing aspect to getting comfortable. Comfort, in and of itself, is not necessarily a bad thing. I'm certainly not saying you have to give up your comfortable mattress to be able to connect with God. But when someone gets comfortable, they tend to forget where that comfort comes from. People dream about having a comfortable life. We even call it "The American Dream."

There was something strangely inspiring about that Puritan prayer above the first time I heard it. So I began to sing it and it became one of my favorite choruses on my first album. It brings out strong reactions in people. I'm finding these two reactions most often:

1. What? *Really?* C'mon. You don't really want to *sing* that!
2. Oh, *yes.* This is the chorus that my church has needed to sing for years. I can't sing it enough. *Break us, Lord!*

Through my conversations with those who are more reactionary, I am finding some things to be consistent. Those who are comfortable in their faith really aren't hip to too much disturbance and disruption in their mojo. I get it.

If things are good, if things are stable, why ask God to save us from these comforts? If it ain't broke, why fix it? If you find something that works, there's nothing wrong with sticking with it.

Then there are those who have a deep desire for something more — more than whatever it is they're searching for. They're singing this chorus until their voices give out. They want the box to be turned upside down — obliterated even.

What is right or wrong depends fully on where you are in your journey. I don't know where that is and wouldn't tell you how to navigate it. But I do know this: I grow in my faith the most when I am disturbed and disrupted. I get spiritually lazy when I'm not.

Those Puritans wanted something extra. Something I don't quite understand. Or didn't until I met Danny.

It was a balmy 32 degrees in downtown Atlanta when DJ Dust — the filmmaker shooting my EPK (electronic press kit) — decided it would be a great idea to do the next segment of the video shoot at 7:00 a.m. in a park downtown. An EPK is simply a promo piece for an upcoming project. So I was able to record videos explaining each and every song coming out on my first record. I was thrilled with the opportunity . . . just not the weather.

The second we got out of the car I could feel the wind racing over my bald head, turning it into a brown ice cube. "Hey, man. There's a wall around the corner here. I absolutely love it. It's bright yellow and where the sun is right now; it's gonna look *sick* on screen." Dust knew what he was doing.

As we were unpacking the gear from the back of the truck I started glancing around at my surroundings. There were pockets of what I assumed were homeless people all over the park, bundled up in their sleeping bags and trying to keep as warm as possible. "Listen, I'm going to turn the car and face it north, in case we have to make a run for it. This isn't the safest of 'hoods," Dust informed the crew. So Dust, myself, Chico (my A&R manager), and Dust's assistant all rolled up to this wall.

Dust sits me down, and it's action time. "You're the God of Second Chances ... You're the God who still romances. We're in awe before you now, and our hearts are crying out ..." I start on the chorus of my song "God of Second Chances." Dust had me sing the chorus about four times through and then stop so I could tell the story behind the song.

I wrote that song because we are *all* in need of second, third, and four-billionth chances. God is a redeemer and will fulfill his promises of grace. It's a song of renewal, redemption, and restoration. And although all I could think about was how absolutely cold it was, the song was warm in my heart.

Just as I was starting the fourth round of singing the chorus, I noticed a man pushing a shopping cart, walking behind the cameras to my left. He didn't even as much as bounce his eyes in our direction, not wanting to make eye contact with those whom he normally is judged by.

As he passed behind Dust, I had a nudge. You know those nudges. The ones you have no choice but to respond to. I'm not gonna get all crazy Holy Spirit on you right now—that's for another book—but this was almost as physical a nudge from the spiritual world as I've ever felt. Call it a prompting if you want. But I felt it. And it nudged me to simply say hello. What harm could come from that?

"Hey, man. What's up?" I asked as I stopped playing my guitar for a moment. The man stopped his cart, cocked his head right, looked at me square in the face, and started walking over. Great.

God, I just wanted to say hey. Nothing else. I don't have room for this conversation, Lord. I'll just give him some money.

So I started digging in my pockets for some change. The closer he got, the more defined his face became. This man has stories ... but I don't have time to hear them. I swear I had a dollar in my pocket. He then spoke. "You singing gospel, man?"

His voice was rich with an island accent. I could almost feel the summer breeze when he spoke even though the freezing wind was biting my bald scalp.

"I said, you singing gospel, man?" he snapped me out of my momentary mirage of warm Jamaican weather, and I replied, "Well, it's not gospel per se. I mean it's Jesus music. So I guess it could be called gospel. But I'm no Kirk Franklin."

"You sing your song, I'll sing mine," he says.

With that, Danny—that was his name—walks up, lowers himself to his knees so that we are eye-to-eye, pulls off his hood, and his Jamaican dreads start dancing on his shoulders. He puts his hands up in the air ... and starts singing with me.

I start back into the chorus.

"You're the God of second chances ... You're the God who still romances!"

Then Brother Danny, in his Rastafarian accent, flows right in after the chorus ...

"One Jah, One Creator, One Father! One Jah, One Creator, One Father!"

On time, on beat, with the lyrical style of a master poet. We begin this lyrical dance. It went on for a good five minutes. Some of my favorite lines Danny inserted into my song:

"Clap your tiny hands for joy. Clap your tiny hands for joy."

"I say he's moving here, he's moving there, he's moving all over the atmosphere!"

It was surreal. I kept looking for John Quiñones to come walking out of the bushes with his ABC film crew from *What Would You Do?* I was lost in the moment of the song ... and his words and his style and his melodies. A Jamaican accent laced in with words about the Holy Spirit moving around the atmosphere and lyrics about clapping your tiny hands for joy. They were so raw yet so soft. I've never in my life felt more spiritually connected to a musical moment than I did right then. I've led worship in the largest churches in the world, have sung on stage with some of the most talented worship leaders on the planet, yet nothing came close to this moment. Nothing came close to this early morning chance encounter with a leathered skin man with piercing eyes named Danny.

I was so wrapped up in the moment that I completely forgot about Dust and Chico. Chico was on his cell phone talking to someone while he was filming with my flip camera. (His whole exchange is out there on YouTube.)

"Yooooo! Yoooooo, man! This is *craaaaazy*! Carlos is singing with this homeless man, and it sounds amazing! Yooooo! Imma call you back."

And just as any filmmaker would, Dust kept shooting ... and shooting. We captured the entire song. It was mind blowing. The moment was invited by a simple hello. And when the music stopped, I thought the moment was over. And I was blessed. Little did I know that I was about to get handed the ultimate gift.

When I stood up to give Danny a hug, he didn't want to let go. He just kept holding me. When we let go I started going Anderson Cooper on him. Where was he from? How did he get here? How long has he been a singer? All of it.

Turns out, Danny was from Jamaica; had some musical background but nothing formal. And he just was on the down and out in the ATL at the moment. At the end of our conversation I locked eyes with Danny and tried to encourage him,

"Keep trying to make it, man. You keep trying to make it. Okay?"

He looked me square in the eye, cocked his head sideways with a confused look on his face, and said, "Trying to make it? No, man. I ain't trying to make it ... I *am* making it. Jah puts his soldiers everywhere. Jah says, 'Yea though you walk through the valley of the shadow of death' ... so he places some of us in that valley."

Game, set, match.

You see here is the real deal: Those of us with our white picket fences, minivans, and savings accounts—we, my friends ... us ... we are the ones who are *trying* to make it. Danny, my new friend, he has *nothing*. So *all* he has to rely on is the generosity of Jesus Christ. *All* he has to rely on is his faith. For every single meal. For every single need. So the look on Danny's face was a look of, "You silly rich man." Because it is so true. All of our stuff. All of our things. All of it. It is just one more thing keeping us relying on ourselves and keeping us from relying on Jesus Christ alone.

Now, am I saying we must all experience a season of homelessness in order for us to actually get it? To actually understand how it feels to be totally dependent on God? Absolutely not.

But what I am saying, and I now understand because of the truth bomb that Brother Danny dropped on me, is this: It's a *lot* harder for those *with* to connect to our God than it is for those *without*. Now I get it.

When we are disturbed and disrupted, we no longer have the routines and the comforts that make us numb to what is around us. We see things fresh again.

Danny afforded me the opportunity to see all the stuff that was getting in the way of my completely depending on Christ alone.

Danny hugged me one last time before grabbing his shopping cart and pushing it south into the heart of the park. When he left we all just kinda stood there with our mouths hanging open. *What just happened?*

We packed up our gear and headed to the next location ... but I couldn't shake Danny from my mind. A few days later I drove back to the same park to look for my new friend. Not a single person had any idea who I was talking about.

Not a single person. I showed everyone in the park a picture and the video of my friend Danny. None of the other homeless men had ever seen him. Danny could have been an angel for all I know. But either way, I know this—Danny gave me a gift that day.

He gave me the gift of a moment that will forever change the way I look at the homeless and the way I chase after God. Danny changed me. And I received his moment with open arms.

Save us from these comforts.
Break us of our need for the familiar.
Spare us any joy that's not of You.
And we will worship You.

The moments we make hold within them the greatest gifts we have in this life, because without them, we miss the point of being here. God put us here to learn how to love each other and to learn how to love him. That comes through *living* on purpose and with purpose. That comes from connecting, learning, loving, giving, losing, failing, and recovering. That comes from creating, receiving, and rescuing. All of that is Moment Making.

It's better that way ...

THE MOMENT-MAKING METHOD

When I was six, being a Moment Maker was a part of my everyday life. I jumped my bike off dirt ramps. I swung on vines across newly discovered creeks. I surprised my mom with flowers from under Mrs. Tarpley's mailbox. I didn't realize that people actually reach a point in life where they hit Cruise—when they let life take the wheel. They let life control their everyday instead of being in charge themselves.

The older we get, the safer we get. And the safer we get, the fewer chances we have for Creating, Receiving, and Rescuing Moments. My friends, Moment Making is not for the faint of heart. It is a journey that takes us out of our comfort zone and leads to a life filled with the kinds of adventures most only dream of having. So, as we've journeyed together through these pages, learning what these moments look like in our lives and the life of the Father, let's spend a little time learning how to intentionally implement this Moment-Making lifestyle into every day.

As we've covered, there are three types of moments: Created Moments, Received Moments, and Rescued Moments. Although these are, on the surface, different, they all share the same principles. As you start building a life of moments, use these four pillars.

1. Understanding

Before we can deliver a moment of value, we must understand why we are making moments in the first place.

When I first started dissecting the lives of great Moment Makers, I saw one common thread. They all understood why they were doing what they were doing.

I remember playing Pin the Tail on the Donkey as a kid.

The way it works is that you are blindfolded, spun around, and then told to place the tail on the backside of the paper donkey. As silly as this sounds, I'm sure you remember how much fun it was when some of the kids would pin the tail right between that donkey's eyes.

Sometimes when it comes to our Moment Making we have this same approach — no direction, just close your eyes and aim. This isn't Moment Making. Moment Making is much more intentional.

We first need to understand *why* this moment is going to happen.

- In Created Moments we must understand *why* this moment will make someone else's life better.
- In Received Moments we must understand *why* this moment will make our life better.
- In Rescued Moments we must understand *why* this moment is in need of rescue in the first place.

It is important to come to a place of understanding before moments can be worth the time and effort.

Over the past decade or so bucket lists have become all the rage because they are filled with dreams. Sadly, people often take the time to compile this list of forty things they want to do before they die and end up only marking off a few. The biggest reason this happens is because they don't know *why* they put those things on the list in the first place. They just fill their buckets with things that will get their hearts racing. And although a racing heart is great, you can go for a run and get your heart racing as well.

So I have this saying ...

Life's too big to fit in a bucket.

If you're truly going to be a Moment Maker, no bucket can contain the number of opportunities there are for making moments. So I ask you to do this one thing ...

Move the *Why* ahead of the Who, What, When, Where, and How.

Remember:

- Once you discover the Why, the moment becomes one worth having.
- Once you discover the Why, someone else will feel valued in the moment you've created.
- Once you discover the Why, you will have the sentence that comes before the exclamation point.

2. Exploring

In a Moment-Making life, *exploring* is what cultivates attentiveness and intentionality.

As a kid, when I was told the story of Christopher Columbus, I remember wondering what he thought the second he set eyes on the Americas. Did he think it was a mirage for a moment? Did he put the anchor down a few miles offshore and simply study what was before him? Did he simply sail to shore with wild abandon? These answers weren't in any of the stories I was told, but I knew that these answers were important. Anyone who has explored anything remembers the first time their eyes and heart connected with a magnificent discovery.

For Moment Makers this step of exploration is crucial in the development of moments.

- Without exploration Created moments fall flat.
- Without exploration Received Moments are missed.
- Without exploration Rescued Moments slip from our grasp.

Exploring is vital in the life of a Moment Maker. I like to simplify this part of the process. I have it down to a science. For me it looks like this:

1. Every day, an alarm goes off on my phone. It's scheduled for three times a day. On the alarm it says: *Explore.* That's it.
2. I stop what I'm doing and tune in my eyes, ears, and heart to the world around me.
3. I open up a notebook, app, or any idea-capturing device and begin to capture what comes.

It's funny how we're so focused on the menial tasks of our days that we miss the majesty all around us. The other day I was at Starbucks when the alarm went off. I thought there cannot be another idea here in this suburban generic coffee shop for a moment to be made.

But because that alarm went off, I went ahead and explored. My eyes went to the side of my cup. We all know that the most recognizable symbol of Starbucks is the Siren on the front of the cup. Although, I'm pretty sure the little boxes where the barista writes your order, your name, and (if you are lucky) a smiley face are just as recognizable as the mermaid. So I snapped a picture of it. I captured the idea and filed it away for a rainy day.

Sometime later, I pulled out that thought, and here's what I did with it: I took my oldest, Sohaila, for a date at Starbucks and had the baristas write four words in those boxes I gave them that described her: *Grace, Compassion, Love, Respect.*

She was halfway through her hot chocolate when she saw the

words, "Daddy? What's this? This is weird right? Why would they write this on here?" This led to a fantastic moment at 3:34 p.m. on a normal Tuesday afternoon. Remember:

Anyone can buy a moment; not everyone can create one.

I have been practicing this exploration technique for four years now. And I have gathered over 34,000 Moment-Making ideas in my Moment-Making folders — no exaggeration. Some examples are images I want to capture, places I want to visit, dates I want to create for my wife.

So you see perfect moments may look like they're made on a moment's notice, but the truth is, without the harvesting of ideas first, you may miss the moment right under your nose! So *explore*, my friends. *Explore.*

3. Pausing

Without the *Pause*, the Why can get lost.

Oh, my friends. Oh, my dear friends. If this is not the antithesis of our culture I don't know what is. We live in a society and time in which pausing is almost a four-letter word. But how can we adequately know the truth of our current situations without the *Pause*?

First, we must understand that life is not a sprint. But it's not a marathon either, because no man knows the last days. No man. Whenever I ask someone how life is going, nine times out of ten they reply with this: "Crazy, man!" or "Slammed. So busy." Those responses are filled with zero Pause. And when we do not Pause, we can't see what is right in front of us. Without a Pause you will find that your aim is off and you can totally miss your mark.

Recently my friends Pete and Blake have been teaching me to hunt. If you are a deer lover or vegetarian, just try to stay with me because the illustration is important.

When I see a deer from the tree stand, I don't grab the rifle and fire away from the hip. No. I slowly place the rifle on the perch, aim down the sight of the scope, and before my finger pulls the trigger back toward me and the bullet flies toward dinner ... I pause. I take a deep breath and on the exhale release the ammunition. If I were to fire without that breath I would miss every single time. The Pause is what centers me to see my target most clearly.

The same can be said about Moment Making. We see most clearly when we pause because it can allow us to see beyond the excitement over the idea to the potential flaws in the execution:

- You want to *create* a moment by proposing to your girlfriend during the halftime of the Bulls game, but you never bothered to learn that she is (a) a fan of basketball or (b) afraid of crowds.
- You encounter a *received* moment when the gift of the moment isn't over yet; there are new truths to uncover; but you have hurried on to the next moment without stopping to see what else is there for you.
- You realize a moment is in need of *rescue*, but rather than taking a step back to see what really could salvage this moment, you barrel through and force something that may only make the situation worse.

I have told you of the thousands of ideas I have at my disposal. Ready to make a moment at a moment's notice, if you will. But rushing into a moment without pausing to understand the Why and to explore the possibilities will usually result in a moment in need of rescue. That is taking an average moment and wrapping it in the breath of God. Remember:

Don't be a Moment Taker; be a Moment Maker.

Pausing can lead to a great idea becoming greater.

4. Living

Life happens in moments, and if we aren't paying attention, we will miss what they are really all about.

This is the final stage of Moment Making—the stage where our moments take flight, where our newly formed beliefs take root, the moment where a rescue ends with an experience that is life giving.

It's the part of Moment Making that dreams are made of. This is the fun part. The place where your belly fills with butterflies and your heart soars with joy. We must be deliberate. We must be purposeful.

I can't begin to describe the joy you will feel when you:

- *Create* a moment for the woman you love when she walks across a field to a canopy of roses you have built, not for an engagement or even a birthday, but ... just because;
- *Have a received* moment by choosing to make an entire record with amazing homeless musicians, and loading it onto inexpensive mp3 players and handing them out to a homeless community, letting them know that these songs are not only for them, they are by them;
- *Rescue* a moment by using your own journey through a disappointment or help another person suffering in a similar way to move forward in life as a free man or woman.

These are the moments that life was meant for. And all of this points to the ultimate Moment Maker. Studying Jesus will fill your Moment-Making journey with intention instead of filling a bucket with ideas. This is what a lifestyle of Moment Making boils down to:

Live *with* purpose and *on* purpose.

When you pay attention, you will discover that the opportunity for moments is surrounding you right now. This moment.

ACKNOWLEDGMENTS

My wife told me many years ago ..., "You know, you're a good singer, but you're a great writer."

I didn't know if I should have been offended or grateful.

I now know.

There has been a writer waiting to flow out of these skinny fingers for a long time.

Thank you to my agent, Esther Fedorkevich, for seeing the potential in me and trusting your gut.

Thanks to my writing coach, Cara Highsmith, for holding this rookie author's hand the whole way.

Thank you, Teresa Davis, for seeing the whole picture of who I am.

Thanks to Carolyn McCready and the entire team at Zondervan for helping me share this message of living life.

Oh. And the three Little Whitts.

Sohaila, Seanna, and Losiah.

Thank you for not telling your friends that your daddy spent hours upon hours in the closet with his laptop.

'Cause that would be entirely inappropriate, and your friends would never come over again.

I was writing my book in there. It was the only place I could get away from you kids.

And to all who have kept up with *mi vida loca* on *ragamuffinsoul.com* the last eight years.

What a ride, huh? This book is a reflection of the bravery you guys gave me to share my story with the world.

OK. Time to write the next one ...